INSPIRING, GENUINE

John and Joyce Hanson have been _____ years. Throughout my years of involvemen_____reach, I have observed their unwavering faithfulness. Never have I known anyone more genuine, humble, and committed to God's calling than this couple. Their story, as captured in this book, will inspire and encourage you to lay everything down to pursue what God asks of you.

Stewart K. Farley, Senior Pastor and IMO Board Member
Rhema Christian Center, Lewisburg, West Virginia

DYNAMIC, LACED WITH ADVENTURE . . .

Once I began reading, I could not put this book down! It is extremely well written, and the author has captured the essence of John and Joyce's life story and their calling to the mission field. Flowing with dynamic testimony, laced with some adventure, and always . . . the fulfillment of God's faithfulness, *Harvesting Haiti—Led by the Master* is guaranteed to bless hearts and souls. Within each of His children, God has placed a spiritual desire to make some difference in the lives of others. John and Joyce are the embodiment of that desire.

Dave Hanson, Brother

SUPERB, POWERFUL . . .

This book is a superb account of inspired Christian service. It demonstrates that obedience to God's call is the primary qualifier for powerful ministry. The narrative is filled with firm, practical principles for successful missionary work and should be read by anyone who wishes to minister within a culture other than his or her own.

Donald E. Stelting, Ph.D.
Academic Dean Emeritus, Nazarene Bible College

EXCELLENCE OF SPIRIT . . .

I was 19 years old when I first visited Haiti. Forty-one years of ministry have taken me all across the globe. In all of my travels, I have not found such excellence of doctrine, construction, personnel, spirit, accommodations, and love as I have found in John and Joyce Hanson with International Missions Outreach.

Tommy Bates, Senior Pastor
Community Family Church, Independence, Kentucky

COMPASSIONATE . . .

On a mission trip to Haiti in the early 90's, we fell in love with John and Joyce Hanson and the IMO ministries. Immediately, Fayetteville Community Church began to support IMO. We have continued to support building schools and churches, the Child Sponsorship Program, the Christmas Shoebox Project, and other special projects. IMO is handled with integrity and compassion, and we are proud to be a part of IMO's ministry.

Wesley Pritchard, Pastor and Ken Pritchard, Pastor
Fayetteville Community Church, Fayetteville, North Carolina

ENCOURAGING . . .

It has been my privilege and joy to be a part of the lives and ministry of John and Joyce Hanson. Their commitment, passion, and faithfulness to minister God's love to the people of Haiti are an inspiration to all who are called to the ministry. . . . I know this book will both bless and encourage all who read it to stay faithful to the call of God.

Darrell Huffman, Pastor
New Life Church, Huntington, West Virginia

DEDICATION, COMMITMENT . . .

I have known Missionaries John and Joyce Hanson for 43 years. I have never met a couple more dedicated and committed to the call of God placed on their lives. Only time and eternity will tell how many lives have been changed, both physically and spiritually, because of their obedience.

Roger Ewing, Pastor
White Oak Worship Center, Blairs, Virginia

Harvesting Haiti—
Led by the Master

By John and Joyce Hanson

WRITTEN BY
CHRISTINE BARBETTI-FEAMSTER

WESTBOW
PRESS
A DIVISION OF THOMAS NELSON

Copyright © 2013 Christine Barbetti-Feamster.

All rights reserved. No part of this book may be used or reproduced by any means,
graphic, electronic, or mechanical, including photocopying, recording, taping or by any
information storage retrieval system without the written permission of the publisher
except in the case of brief quotations embodied in critical articles and reviews.

WestBow Press books may be ordered through booksellers or by contacting:

WestBow Press
A Division of Thomas Nelson
1663 Liberty Drive
Bloomington, IN 47403
www.westbowpress.com
1-(866) 928-1240

Because of the dynamic nature of the Internet, any web addresses or links contained in
this book may have changed since publication and may no longer be valid. The views
expressed in this work are solely those of the author and do not necessarily reflect the
views of the publisher, and the publisher hereby disclaims any responsibility for them.

ISBN: 978-1-4497-9148-3 (sc)
ISBN: 978-1-4497-9149-0 (e)

Library of Congress Control Number: 2013906659

Printed in the United States of America.

WestBow Press rev. date: 05/21/2013

To our daughters,
Cynthia (Cindy) Joyce Sheikh and Faithe Ann Claxton,
who willingly gave up a land of comfort for a land of hardships.

*For God is not unjust to forget your work
and labor of love which you have shown toward His name,
in that you have ministered to the saints, and do minister.*

Hebrews 6:10 (NKJV)

Contents

Acknowledgments

No book is written without the help of many key people. Joyce, my dear wife, next to Jesus, is my dearest friend and my greatest love. I thank her for all the input she gave to this book.

As Joyce and I began to recall the memories of how God called us to Haiti, how He provided for us to go to Haiti, and all the wonderful folks who have influenced our lives throughout our ministry in Haiti, it is truly impossible to convey our deepest gratitude. She and I have been on this journey in Haiti for more than 40 years, and God has blessed us beyond belief. So, I want to acknowledge some of those special people who have journeyed with us, supported us, encouraged us, prayed for us, as well as those who have been instrumental in getting our story published. It is with my deepest appreciation that I acknowledge the following persons:

> Our daughter, Faithe, and our late daughter, Cindy. Both of you have brought so much joy into our lives. You are special treasures to us. Thank you for

sharing the call of God and assisting and giving of yourselves.

William and Mildred Hanson, my mother and father. You raised us and taught us from our youth the ways of Jesus and that we are not our own, because we were bought by His blood. Even though you are in heaven now, we thank you for your love to us.

Derrel and Betty Friend, Hulda (Mama) Huff, Ed and Donna Unicume, David and Ora Mae Simpkins, dear friends. You believed in us and stood by us from the very beginning of our ministry. We could never forget your love, and we thank you.

IMO Advisory Board Members: Rev. Jim Boggess, Rev. Ed Davis, Rev. Roger Ewing, Rev. Stewart Farley, Rev. David Gourley, Mr. David Hanson, Rev. Jerry Haynes, Rev. David Hodge, Rev. Sammy Huff, Rev. Darrell Huffman, Mr. Keven Kemerer, Dr. Jim Mears, Rev. Bill Morris, Rev, Ken Pritchard, Dr. Jon Sullivan, and Rev. Michael Tackett. We are so grateful for your sacrificial dedication and support throughout the years.

Christine Barbetti-Feamster, writer. You encouraged us throughout your writing of our story, and you would not let us quit. Your endless work of writing, rewriting, editing, finding and working with a publisher has made it possible for our story to be told. Joyce and I thank you for caring for us and for God's great work in Haiti.

Pam Stelting, editor. You have done a wonderful job

in making all of our rough edges smooth and crossing all of our T's and dotting all of our I's. Your labor of love shines brightly in our finished work.

All the many pastors, churches, and supporters who have helped make International Missions Outreach what it is today. We appreciate each of you so very much, and we thank God for you.

Our extended Haitian Family, whom we love dearly. You welcomed us with open arms and have worked with us together in serving Jesus. Thank you for sharing the passion that we have to win souls for the Kingdom of God. We love you with an everlasting love.

Most importantly, our sincere gratitude to our Lord Jesus can not be adequately expressed by words. We acknowledge all You have done for us and for our Haitian brothers and sisters. We love You more than we will ever be able to express. We will love You and serve You forever.

John and Joyce Hanson

Prologue

Swing the sickle, for the harvest is ripe. Joel 3:13 (NIV)

The view of the ocean, the mountains, and the city of Port-au-Prince from the fourth story open observation deck at our headquarters in Delmas is so powerful! Delmas, a suburb of the largest city in Haiti, Port-au-Prince, is where our visitors and volunteers stay when they come to Haiti. After they arrive, the first thing I suggest they do is to, "Go climb the steps to the observation deck and see the majesty of what God has created."

Looking eastward from the rooftop, we can watch the dawning of the morning and feel the warmth and excitement of a new day. As the sun begins its upward climb, it awakens the city ever so gently. At this high elevation, the ever-present poverty I know exists throughout the city seems to disappear. Toward the south, the mountains of Boutilier are dotted with houses and hotels where tourists come to relax and enjoy the mountain breezes. It was in this area of La Boule, in 1976, where we made our first home with our two daughters, Cindy and Faithe. I always remember fondly those blessed evenings spent playing Monopoly and laughing with our young girls.

The northern view shows the mountain road that leads to the village of Terre Rouge, where we just built a new church and a new school. Since 1945, when a few of the families in the community of Terre Rouge started having church services in a small outstation, these families have been waiting patiently for a permanent building. The westward view of the ocean is my favorite. In the evening when the sun starts its downward slide, the sky stretches out in brilliant hues of red, orange, and yellow, as the rays travel though the hazy evening sky. When that huge ball of fire finally sets over the sea and drops out of sight, it seems to fall right into the ocean itself.

Sometimes I climb the steps to the observation deck just to think and clear my mind of all the activity happening below. There is something calming and refreshing, yet energizing, about being out in the open with nothing between you and the heavens. Looking down on all the activity happening around the church, the elementary school, the Bible school, the warehouse, the guest quarters, and the service center located at our headquarters, my mind's eye pictures another view in another time.

I see the property as it was 30 years ago when we purchased it—an ex-cornfield turned trash dump for the neighborhood. Covered in weeds and debris from years of being a convenient garbage catch-all for the surrounding properties, our land was as ugly as ugly gets. I had hired a few workers to help clear away the heaps of garbage and discarded junk, but clearing the land went slowly. We only had a couple of rakes and hoes, so most of the work was done by hand. As I labored with the men day after day in the sweltering heat, I noticed that none of them ever brought anything to eat. In fact, only a few of them ever brought any water. I felt guilty eating the lunch Joyce fixed for me each morning. It disturbed me a whole lot that these hard workers would come early in the morning and work till sundown with only a little bit of water to drink that we borrowed from a neighbor's well. And the fact they had nothing at all to eat, well, that just about broke my heart.

One day I could take it no longer. I gave Panyel a few dollars to go and buy some rice so we could feed the workers. Panyel, a small, quiet-spoken Haitian, with the kindest eyes I had ever seen, was one of the workers who had given his heart to the Lord in the early beginnings of our ministry. He had already proven to be a valuable worker at our house in Mariane. When Panyel came back with a bag of rice and tomato paste, we were still no closer to feeding the workers as we had neither a pot nor a stove with firewood to cook the rice.

The next day, I scrounged up a large iron pot, and Panyel found three flat white rocks and put them together so he could set the pot upon them. We were almost there but what to use for firewood? If I had been in the mountains of West Virginia, firewood wouldn't have been a problem. But in Haiti, well, wood is like gold—maybe better than gold—and just as scarce. If wood is needed, it is imported from the States. Many years ago, most all trees of any size had been cut down and used either for construction or firewood, so finding firewood on this large island was a major problem.

At first, Panyel found some small twigs and sticks to burn in his makeshift stove, but that soon disappeared. As I was pondering this dilemma, Panyel left and returned a time later dragging a huge wooden statute. I remembered that statue because on his last visit to Haiti, Pastor Sammy Huff, from Michigan, had purchased it from some Haitian vendor with the intention of taking it back to the States for his office. Because it was too large to carry on the plane and too large to ship by mail, he asked us to store it for him until he could figure out some way to get it back to the States. And here was Panyel offering it up as a sacrifice to do the Lord's work!

Each day, little by little, Panyel cut up the large wooden statue and used it to build his fire to cook the rice for the workers. Some days Panyel would buy beans and cook them over his outdoor "grill." Neither the rice nor the beans were much of a lunch to me, but the workers were appreciative, and the work got done. When Pastor Sammy returned to Haiti a few months later, he asked about his statue. With a twinkle in his eyes, all Panyel could say to him was, "It went up in smoke!"

Clearing the land was long and difficult—so long that it became discouraging to watch. Oh, to have a bulldozer or backhoe for just one day! I remember the day I sat down beside Panyel and saw the tiredness and discouragement in his eyes. It was then I felt led to share with him the vision the Lord had given to me about this property.

"You see this land here, Panyel," I said to him. "One day it will be used as a work for the Lord, and there will be a large mission here. And through it all, you will still be here, and you will be over all the workers."

Panyel stared back at me strangely as though I were speaking in a foreign tongue; it was something he could not comprehend. But I had no doubt that God had given me that vision, for I saw it clearly.

Now, looking down from the fourth story observation deck atop our visitor's quarters, the nice third floor apartment Joyce and I share, and the ground floor storage facility, I also see our Delmas Church to the right. It is the largest of all our Haitian churches. The Delmas Elementary School shares some of its rooms with the church, and in the schoolyard are dozens of children playing kickball and some of their favorite Haitian games. On the right behind the church, I see the Bible school where future pastors and lay ministers are milling around waiting for classes to start. The aroma of fresh coffee brewing in the morning air tells me the cooks have already started preparing food for the school children's lunches. Throughout our 18 schools, we feed over 5,000 children every day.

Directly in front of me, I see the maintenance shed where all the vehicles and machinery are housed and serviced. This is where volunteer workers have spent many hours building pews, tables, and desks for each new church and school. Also, to the left, I see the recently built, 14,000-square-foot warehouse with loading dock and drive-in door. Here, we store all the supplies brought in by containers across the ocean, sent by churches and individuals who have pledged their support. To the right of the warehouse are three furnished, one-room efficiency apartments with kitchenette and bath for volunteers who have come to work for a week or more to share in God's work in Haiti. A new 12-foot-high wall surrounds our small, gated community.

Today, Panyel carries the keys to every building on the property. Every summer when Joyce and I go to the States to raise money for International Missions Outreach, Panyel is the one left in charge. The vision God gave me came true. Looking down on the property now, it is easy to see proof of the vision God revealed to me. But way, way back in the beginning years before it all came to pass, I had lots of questions about that vision God revealed to me. Oh, I didn't have any lack of faith that God could bring it all to pass; I was very familiar with the God I served, and I knew He could do *any* and *all* things.

Yes, I knew my God was capable. But my toughest question for God was, "How can You use me, a coal miner's son from the hills of West Virginia, to make it all come to pass . . . ?"

CHAPTER 1

Growing Up in West Virginia

He who gathers crops in summer is a prudent son, but he who sleeps during harvest is a disgraceful son. Proverbs 10:5 (NIV)

MY MAMA NAMED me John Paul the day I was born in February 1943. Whether it was a foreshadowing of what was to come my way or not, I really can't say. But I can assure you those are two impossible missionary names to live up to. My dad wasn't around on the day of my birth as he had been shipped off to Germany in Europe to help fight World War II. So, Mama got to pick my names out all by herself.

By the time of my birth, my parents, Mildred and Bill Hanson, already had three other children: Billy, sister India, and Buck. And they weren't finished when I came along. Four years after me came brother Charlie and then the baby of the family, David, who was also given a beloved biblical name by my mom.

My hometown of Queen Shoals, West Virginia, located about four miles north of Clendenin on Route 4, is about as pretty as it gets in small-town USA. Beautiful lush, green mountains, plenty of forests with streams and rivers to skip rocks and skinny dip—what more does a young boy need? Queen Shoals, situated in Kanawha County in southern central West Virginia, is just a few miles from Charleston, the state capital. The mighty Elk River, the longest river in West Virginia that flows entirely within the state's boundaries, runs through my hometown. The town's name came from the queenly sand bars—shoals—along that river. It was *on* and *in* that river where my brothers and I spent most of our time growing up. Many a day found us swimming along the shoals. If we weren't swimming or building rafts or jon boats to use for fishing, our homemade fishing poles were catching blue gills or sunfish to bait our trotlines. With our trotlines we loved to catch the plentiful catfish that swam in the Elk River.

We boys couldn't wait for school to be out so we could spend all our spare moments each day exploring the many wonders of Elk River. My brothers and I would spread the word to our friends in the neighborhood that we were heading to the woods, and off we would go into the Appalachian Mountains that surrounded our small town. We built crude log cabins and campfires sometimes right on the river, if we found a good swimming hole there. At night, in those dark mountains, a huge campfire was a necessity for telling tall tales and ghost stories. The eerie night sounds of the woods and its creatures weren't quite so scary, if you could see what was happening all around you.

Cookin' wasn't a manly thing to do back then, but since no girls were allowed in our select group of fellows, we brought the easiest thing we could think of to feed our ever-hungry stomachs—bologna and a can of pork n' beans. The beans didn't take much fixin' and anyone can slap a couple pieces of bread together with bologna in the middle. To this day, pork n' beans and bologna are my favorite snack foods. Yep, they're comfort food that fills the stomach and makes the heart light! It probably sounds a wee bit corny or idealistic, but Queen

Shoals was an adventurer's paradise, a natural haven, and a small piece of heaven where this boy delighted in all it had to offer.

Family life was simple for us. Because Mom and Dad were devoted totally to God and church, we spent a great deal of time in church. As a lay minister, Dad opened and closed the church doors a lot, always taking his family with him. It was never a matter of whether we kids were going to church or not; we knew if the doors were open, we were there. Every time! I can't ever remember staying home, because we never had any excuses for not going that were good enough for Dad.

During the warm summer months, we were in church somewhere just about every night. Back then, revivals were not the short "instant revivals" of today. Our meetings would go on for two or three weeks at the least and sometimes as long as five or six weeks. People were hungry for the presence and move of the Lord. When the evangelist gave the salvation invitation, people came running and weeping to the altar and stayed until they had "prayed through." "Praying through" meant another soul's name was written in the Lamb's Book of Life, and there was a great deal of praising the Lord in singing and shouting when a sinner had come home.

Going to church wasn't optional and neither were family devotions. Mom and Dad weren't just "church" Christians; they were Christians *all* the time. Every evening as the day came to a close, without fail, Dad gathered us all in the living room to read a chapter or two from the Bible. Although Dad owned a coal mining business, he was also a lay preacher who helped fill in for the pastor when he couldn't be at church. After the Bible reading was finished, Dad prayed. Mom was next, brother Billy took his turn, and on down the sibling line until we all had a chance to talk with God. Dad encouraged us to pray for whatever we desired and always allowed us to take as long as we wanted. On some evenings when it became my turn to pray, I was asleep. Usually a nudge or a sharp jab from Charlie or Buck kept me from getting on Dad's bad side.

The best prayer in our family was our baby brother, David. He loved to pray and pray and pray and pray. When he ran out of people he knew to pray for, he started praying for all the cats and dogs in the neighborhood. Sometimes he would even include the wild squirrels and rabbits. Personally, I thought he just loved all the attention he was getting at the time. But it's not surprising today that brother Dave is the one sibling who keeps us all connected as a family with his caring, "mothering" instincts. I wouldn't be surprised if he prayed for all of us every night! From those daily family devotions and our church going, my siblings and I were given a strong foundation in Christ—a foundation that has stood the tests of time.

CHAPTER 2

Faith and the Family Business

As long as the earth endures, seedtime and harvest,
cold and heat, summer and winter, day and night
will never cease." Genesis 8:22 (NIV)

MY GRANDPA HANSON owned the J. W. Hanson Coal Company, which had several mines in the Queen Shoals area along with mines in Pups Creek and Cobb Station. All were within the Kanawha Coal Fields area. He also owned a few strip mines out in the Bomont area. When Dad came back from the service in 1945, he went to work fulltime for Grandpa, and then it became the J. W. Hanson & Son Coal Company. Actually, it was pretty much a family affair as Dad's brothers also worked driving coal trucks and loading railroad cars.

We had the usual coal miner's company store that Tennessee Ernie Ford made popular back in the 60s with the big hit, "*Sixteen Tons.*" The miners were paid with our own particular type of script that enabled them to purchase food, clothing, and just about anything else a body might need. I still have a few pieces of that script today. Company stores were established because mine owners didn't like a large amount of cash on hand due to the fear of being robbed. As a young boy, I don't remember anyone complaining about "owing my soul to the company store." Most men were happy just to have a job so they could take care of their families.

Since the late 1700s, West Virginia has always been synonymous with coal. There is a legitimate reason why: 53 of the 55 counties in West Virginia have been blessed with enormous reserves of energy rich bituminous coal. Underlying the topography of the state are 62 individual seams of coal considered economically minable.[1] With this type of sub-surface, it is no wonder numerous coal companies flourished during the 19th and 20th centuries in western Virginia, which later became West Virginia in 1863, during the Civil War. By 1947, West Virginia had reached its peak in coal production producing over 173,653,816 tons in one year.[2] My grandfather's mines contributed greatly to that enormous total.

I really loved working around and in the coal mines. After school, weekends, and then during the summer months, I worked loading mine posts and 2 in. x 8 ft. headers that were used to support the mines' roofs. Just for fun, I would jump on the main line motorcar as it came out of the mines and ride on top of the coal car until it reached the tipple area where the coal would be weighed and dumped into the tipple. From there the coal truck took it to the larger distribution tipple at the railroad. Once at the railroad, the coal would be loaded into the rail cars.

The tipple area of the railroad yards is another area where I worked as a young boy during the summer when school was out. Working around those conveyors and the huge rail cars that were loaded with coal were not exactly safe places for a young child. State and federal mine inspectors occasionally chastised my dad for letting me work in this area stating I was too small and too young. I was also too young to drive the coal trucks when I came home from school each afternoon. However, I was pretty persuasive in getting the truck driver (usually one of my uncles) to let me take the wheel and drive up the dirt roads to the mines. I really loved doing that! Today, none of this would be allowed, and certainly, mine owners would be fined if caught allowing these flagrant violations. Back then, however, it was a different era in the coal mining business, and Grandpa and Dad kept a close eye on us kids, never allowing us to do anything they didn't think we could handle.

If I close my eyes, I can smell coal. Even after my wife, Joyce, and I married, I worked a few years in the mines loading coal during the day and then doubling back in the evening to help cut coal. Despite the dangers, I loved the smell, the constant activity, and the excitement of seeing another load go from deep down in the mountain to atop a rail car on its way to some unknown destination. One could say that coal dust flowed through my veins.

For the most part, coal miners in that era were a hard-working breed of people—good, God-fearing, family-loving people. While working in those mines, I met some of the greatest people I have ever known. Memories from those days are pleasant and comforting.

During the 50s and 60s, with the United States finally recovering from the great depression of the 30s and from World War II in the 40s, the future of coal became uncertain. King Coal, as it was referred to in West Virginia, no longer reigned throughout the Appalachia area; other forms of energy, such as electricity, heating oils, and natural gas, began replacing the once precious black gold. During this time, numerous mines were closed, and miners were forced to move out of the area to find work. Because of the mine closings, the southern counties of West Virginia lost about one-third of their population.[3]

By 1957, Dad was running the coal company by himself, and with the declining demand for coal, Dad struggled to keep the mines open. He hung on until 1964, when he completely shut down the whole coal operation. When he closed the coal mines, coal was selling for about 75 cents a ton, and no one could make any money at that price. With the mines closed, Dad had no money coming in. He worked at odd construction jobs as best he could, but he had a family to support, and he had to pay off overdue bills from the mining company.

It was during this time I began to question some of the ways in which God works. Where were all those people my dad had helped when his business was thriving? It was a commonplace occurrence for my dad to build a house for a pastor or outfit a new pastor's home with furniture. Dad was always the first one to give when a need had to be met for a fellow worker or friend or for an itinerant pastor or missionary passing through our small town. Now, our family was really going through a rough period, and help didn't seem to be coming our way.

Dad was faithful in giving his tithes to the church. And he taught us it was not enough just to tithe, but that God wanted us to be givers also. So, why wasn't God using some of these people to help Dad now? The injustice of it all just seemed to rub me the wrong way. Was the Christian doctrine of reaping what you sow really true?

Through all our hardships, I learned that God doesn't always work in ways I expect Him to. God has His own perfect way of doing things, and He wants us to live by faith, not by what we expect others to do. Dad had lots of faith, and he kept on working and believing that God would take care of him and his family. And God did.

In the 60s, a new industrial era was beginning to emerge in West Virginia. After years of knowing nothing but coal mining, we Hansons were forced to move on to something else. Working with Grandpa and Dad during my youth, I learned much about life. The coal mines, the construction business, working and serving in church, our family life—all were just a training ground for the work God had called us to do in Haiti. Little did I know that, someday, I would use *all* the training I ever had to preach the Gospel of Christ to the nation of Haiti.

CHAPTER 3

Salvation has Come to My House

*But now that you have been set free from sin and have
become slaves to God, the benefit you reap leads to holiness,
and the result is eternal life. Romans 6:22 (NIV)*

Mom and Dad had both given their hearts to the Lord in a Methodist church before they were married, so we kids thought spending lots of evenings and Sundays in church was a normal thing. It was all we knew growing up.

For most of my young life, I pretty much took it for granted that my relationship with God was in good standing, since my parents had brought us up right and took us

High School Photo

to church. However, just to be on the safe side, I would make that trip to the altar just about every time an evangelist preached his sermon on hell. Fire and brimstone so hot it could burn your shirttail! I made many a trip to the altar that way, scared for my eternal safety. But before long (and sometimes I didn't last a week), I would find myself doing something I knew I shouldn't be doing.

All the preachers I knew preached clean living, and that meant doing absolutely nothing that would be displeasing to God. Somehow I always managed *not* to live up to their standards. In my youthful ignorance of our loving God, I thought being a Christian meant living a perfect life. And every time I messed up, I needed to go back to God and ask for my salvation all over again. How wonderful was the day when I finally learned that my salvation was not that fragile!

The summer I was 16, Rev. Earnest Barley, from Mount Hope, West Virginia, came to the old Queen Shoals Tabernacle to hold a revival. I had no indication that this revival would be any different from all the other revivals I had attended with my dad and Rev. Barley throughout the years. Several years previously, Dad had met Rev. Barley through a local radio program. They became friends and were fellow preachers together at many tent meetings and revival services held in our area.

As usual, this revival began during the Sunday evening service and continued on during the weekday evenings. Services had been full of people singing and praising God. Several sinners had confessed their sins, and things were going along mighty good for the Lord and Evangelist Barley. The revival was drawing to a close that Friday evening. There I sat on the back row with Joyce (my girlfriend at the time) listening to the sermon Rev. Barley had titled "*Never A Man Spake Like This Man.*"

His sermon was taken from St. John, chapter 7, where the Jewish leaders—the chief priests and Pharisees—had sent out spies, who were actually temple guards, among the people to bring Jesus in so they could accuse Him of blasphemy or any other Jewish law-breaking act which would entitle them to jail or execute Him. At this point, the leaders were willing to do about anything to silence this radical and remove His influence from their synagogues. But when the temple guards returned to the leaders, they did not have Jesus in tow with them. Furious at their failure, the leaders asked, "Why didn't you bring Him in?" One guard's simple reply was, "No one ever spoke the way this man does."

Maybe, for the first time in my young life, my mind was actually listening to what this man of God was saying to me. I was not fearful of hell but interested in Jesus. I got the overpowering feeling God, or this Jesus, was speaking directly to me through Rev. Barley. The desire to actually know about Jesus and to find out what was different about Him began building in my spirit.

When the Holy Spirit is wooing you, your mind gets quiet. I was not thinking of anything but what that speaker was saying; everything else going on in my life was not important at that moment. The Holy Spirit is such a gentle Being, and the wooing process is so sweet. It was as if I could actually feel God's love surrounding me, pleading with me to come and get to know Him.

The longer Rev. Barley preached, the more the longing to know the real Christ began swelling up within my spirit. By the time the pianist began playing *"Just As I Am"* that Friday evening, I was ready to make that first step down to the altar—just as I was, sin and all. And when I did, Jesus Christ became a reality to me. No longer was Jesus just a name I had heard my father talk about or a name that required me to be good. That night, Jesus became a real person to me, a person who changed my life so drastically that I sold out to Him totally and completely!

This last salvation trip to the altar became my last one. Since that night, I have never wanted to go back and undo that commitment, because when you have a real encounter with Jesus Christ, you will never be the same again.

After my total commitment, going to church was no longer a thing I did because Mom and Dad made me go. I went because I wanted to learn more about Jesus the Man to whom I had surrendered myself. I needed to know how best I could serve in His kingdom, and most of all I wanted to know what He had planned for my life.

CHAPTER 4

A Helpmate for John

*And Ruth the Moabite said to Naomi, "Let me go to the fields
and pick up the leftover grain behind anyone in whose eyes
I find favor. . . . So she went out, entered a field and began
to glean behind the harvesters." Ruth 2:2, 3 (NIV)*

PROCIOUS, WEST VIRGINIA, is a small town between Clay and Clendenin off Route 4 where I, Joyce Louise Nicholson, was born to Mary Marie Lewellyn Nicholson and Eugene Warden Nicholson on January 30, 1944. Originally from Harrisville, West Virginia, my parents migrated to Procious when my dad went to work for the local gas company.

Mom used to say she had three kids by the time she was 19. What she

High School Photo

meant was that Dad's mother had died while he was in the service during World War II, and when Mom married him, she took on the care of his three younger brothers. So, she became an instant mother at an early age. Then on top of that, she began having her own family as well. There for a while, we were all a pretty big crew. Deloris was my oldest sibling, and after me, there were three more children: Michael, my only brother, then Deborah and Pamela. We were a close-knit family with a stay-at-home mom who had her work cut out for her from the day she said, "I do."

We lived on a small, 32-acre farm that was mostly hilly countryside, as were a lot of farms in West Virginia. We had the usual chickens, pigs, and token cow to provide food and milk for us growing kids. We grew our own vegetables in a garden Dad planted down by the river bottom below our home. River-bottom land always makes the best gardens. In the summer, Mom and we girls performed our usual ritual of canning vegetables until the last tomato had been picked and the garden plants had gone to seed.

Along with working fulltime at the local natural gas company, Dad was an auto mechanic in his spare time. To earn a little extra money to support his large family, Dad worked on other peoples' vehicles, and he would mow hay or anything else someone needed him to do to supplement his salary. We children attended Dulles Creek Elementary School and then Clay High School. We were a comfortable family, living with a regular income. Society probably considered us middle class at that time.

There was not a lot of social life for a teenager in Procious, so we went to Clendenin, about 12 miles south of Procious, to a roller skating rink that was open every night and on weekends. Since Clendenin was one of the larger towns in the area, anyone wanting to socialize came from all the smaller towns to congregate at the rink. Young people socializing is a custom as old as the hills in West Virginia, and I was all for that custom! I loved hanging out with my girlfriends at the rink, and it was fun to meet new people.

I was a sophomore in high school the Sunday afternoon John came into the skating rink. I noticed him eyeing me, and it wasn't long before he came over and asked me to skate with him. At the time, I didn't know anything about him or his family. I can't remember the name of the song we skated to, but I did know I liked this tall, clean-cut guy whose personality oozed with confidence and whose touch of the hand made me feel giddy inside. Oh, he was good looking too, and that made it pretty easy to give him my full attention. Even at age 16, John was a force to be reckoned with—never arrogant, but definitely someone who knew who he was and what he liked. And he liked me!

People have always been drawn to John immediately, wherever he goes. Some people call it charisma, but I just call it God's anointing on him. When John took my hand to skate with him, I sensed there was something different and special about this man, and I wanted to find out what it was.

That skate-dance was the first event of our courting days, and we spent every spare moment we had with each other. Of course, with his father being a lay pastor, most of that time spent together was in church. My family went to church, so I was used to spending time in church. I had given my heart to the Lord during a service when I was very young (maybe around ten or so), but I wouldn't say I was serving God with my whole heart at this time. Like most girls my age, I was more interested in dating and marriage than anything else. I also found out that John's father owned several coal mines in the area. I really had no idea he came from such a prosperous family!

John and I fell in love, and with our parents' permission, we planned to marry the next June. We were really very young, but for that day and time, it was not uncommon for people our age to marry. Still, some family members and friends were very negative about our marriage. Most of them thought we were too young to marry. Some of them even told us right out that our marriage would never last. Looking back, I can easily see why they were so negative about our getting married. Marriage is tough, and regardless of what age you are, only the truly committed will stay together. But back then, I was in love, and I had no doubt that John was the man I wanted to be with the rest of my life. A friend of John's, who was with him at the skating rink that afternoon we met, later confided in me that John told him that day, "Joyce is the gal I'm going to marry!"

One Friday evening, John and I were attending a revival service at the old Queen Shoals Tabernacle. The guest evangelist, Rev. Earnest Barley, was a good friend and fellow pastor of John's father. Wedding plans were in the future for John and me, but we both knew something more important had to take place before a wedding. I will never forget the sermon that evening titled, "*Never a Man Spake As This Man.*" The convicting power of the Holy Spirit was flowing in our direction, and I could feel Him dealing with me. I also sensed something powerful was going on with John too. When it came time for the altar call, John took my hand, and we both walked down the aisle to commit our lives together in serving Christ. We both wanted to start out our life together in the unity of Christ. From that time forward, John and I have cherished our commitment to God. That doesn't mean we haven't failed, it just means we have never given up and have never let go of our Savior's hand.

That night, I promised John I would be his helpmate, supporting him in whatever God had planned for his life. I was so much in love with John, it was an easy promise to make. I really had no idea what direction God's plan for our lives would take us, but I knew I wanted to be with John on that journey.

John and Joyce cutting their wedding cake

CHAPTER 5

Preparing our Hearts

The harvest is past, the summer has ended, and
we are not saved. Jeremiah 8:20 (NIV)

FOR THE FIRST year of our marriage, I worked at the coal company during the day. Then, every night, I drove to Charleston, over 25 miles away, to finish out my last year of high school. After I graduated from high school, I worked fulltime in the mines, but the price of coal began to decline. It became increasingly difficult for Dad to make a living in the coal industry. We were selling coal to chemical plants in South Charleston and Institute, loading 15 railroad cars with 75 tons of coal each day. As the cost of coal kept dropping, I knew it was time to find some steady employment. By this time, Joyce had given birth to our first daughter, Cindy, and I now had to provide for three.

After graduation from high school, I found a job with the local gas company for 11 months but was laid off before I had finished my first year. It seemed the gas company policy was to lay you off shortly before your first year ended so you would not be eligible for company benefits. It was cheaper to hire someone new and train them than to keep a current employee and pay their benefits. After my layoff, I found work in construction, which was only temporary due to our severe winters.

With hundreds of coal miners out of work, finding a fulltime, good-paying job in West Virginia was tough. The unemployment rate was skyrocketing in the early 60s because of all the coal mine closings, so I decided to try to find work in Florida. Florida was a familiar place for our family as Dad took us there every year on vacation; I also had a friend who was fortunate enough to have found work there.

Joyce and I decided that I would take off alone and scout out the job situation, and she and Cindy would follow me when I found a job. It did not take long before I found a job in Melbourne, Florida, at a Winn Dixie Store in the meat department. I met with Mr. Walton, the district manager of Winn Dixie, who interviewed me for a meat cutter's job. When he asked me if I had ever cut meat, I had to reply, "No, but I could learn." He hired me. Once I had money coming in, I was anxious for Joyce and Cindy to join me. I loved those two gals with all my heart, and to be apart from them made my heart ache.

Joyce began packing to move to Florida once she knew I had a job. We sold most of our possessions, and Joyce and Cindy took the two-day journey on a Greyhound Bus to begin their new life in Florida. There is a story Joyce likes to tell about her bus trip to Florida that I like too. It proves God cares about everything in our lives. Here is how Joyce tells the story:

> It was difficult selling or giving away just about everything we owned and then moving to a strange new place. I had seldom been far from my hometown, much less moving to another state hundreds of miles

away. I was lonely, scared, and anxious over our move, and I was solely responsible for the care and safety of our two-year-old child.

I knew the journey would be long, so I packed everything I thought I would need for Cindy and me for the two-day trip. The first night on the bus, I realized I had forgotten to pack any juice for Cindy's goodnight drink. We had a ritual at our house where John and I would go in and tuck Cindy in for the night and sometimes read her a story, give her a cup of juice to drink, and kiss her goodnight. But this evening on the bus, when I tried to get her to go to sleep, she just cried for her juice.

There was a gentleman sitting in front of us who I guess had heard Cindy crying. At the next stop, he got off and came back carrying a small bottle of juice. After he gave her the juice, she went to sleep. God knew I did not have the money to spend for that juice, and He found a way to provide it for me through a complete stranger. That small act of kindness bolstered my spirits, because God was letting me know that even our smallest desires are important to Him. I knew if He cared about the small things, He would surely care about our traveling hundreds of miles from home to find a way to make a living.

While working at Winn Dixie, I continued to look for a better paying job. Before long, I found a good one with Pan American World Airways in the maintenance department at the Space Center at Cape Canaveral, Florida. After working there a couple of years, the space program was hit hard by the declining economy. There were severe cutbacks, and once again, I joined the ranks of the unemployed.

It was during this time our second daughter, Faithe, was born. She was such a tiny thing with a head full of beautiful black hair. After looking for work in Florida and finding nothing, we loaded up our 1957 Ford and headed back north to West Virginia. Cindy slept in the back seat, and Joyce put Faithe on a pillow between us in the front seat. We did not have special child carriers back in those days; we didn't even have seat belts! I guess we just trusted God to keep safe the two most precious things in this world to us. After all was said and done, Joyce and I found ourselves back where we started, struggling once again to find work. All my efforts to better myself and provide for my family had failed.

By the time we returned to West Virginia, the Vietnam War was raging and in full bloom. As always, war does create jobs. I was fortunate enough to find employment with Food Machinery Company (FMC) at the Naval Ordinance Plant in South Charleston, West Virginia. I worked the midnight shift, and every night, it was my job to install the inside equipment on the "one thirteen" (113) personnel carrier. These were armored tank vehicles being sent to Vietnam to be used in combat.

My brother, Buck, was not as fortunate as I was, and he took off to Alexandria, Virginia, to look for work. While living in Alexandria, Buck had gotten mixed up in a Pentecostal church. He had come home telling all his family about receiving the baptism in the Holy Ghost and all the different experiences he had encountered up there in that "holy roller" church.

I have to be honest here. I had no desire to listen to him talking about being filled with the Holy Ghost or any stories connected with the experience. All I knew was what I had heard all my life that "speaking in tongues" was of the devil. Being filled with the Holy Spirit was good, but forget the tongues. We were Methodist, and Methodists do not speak in tongues! You have to understand, we were a full-gospel church but not a Pentecostal church.

No one in the family was particularly listening to Brother Buck, but he kept on telling us about the Holy Spirit, planting the seed. Then shortly afterwards, a young couple from Phoenix City, Alabama, Frank and Barbara Abrams, held a two-week revival at my dad's church, the New Queen Shoals Tabernacle. Every night, Evangelist Abrams preached a mighty sermon, and before the night was over, he somehow included in the sermon about how everyone who was saved should be filled with the Holy Spirit. We went to service every night, and the more he preached about the Holy Spirit, the hungrier I got for the infilling of the Holy Spirit. By the second week, I was ready. I told Joyce not to pack a lunch for me when I went to work at night, because I was going to fast and pray all week long.

I did just that—I prayed and fasted all week long. I thought if the infilling of the Holy Spirit was for us today like it was for the disciples and workers who tarried and prayed in the Upper Room, then I wanted it. I read all the Scriptures I could find on the Holy Ghost and continued to attend the revival every night. One thing I have learned about God in the 50 plus years I have served Him is when you get serious about what you want from God, He gets serious with you!

Evangelist Abrams' Friday night sermon was taken from Acts 19, where Paul had arrived in Ephesus, and finding the disciples, he asked them, "Have you received the Holy Ghost since you believed?" I couldn't wait until the sermon was over so I could run to the altar. As I stood there at the altar, Rev. Abrams asked me what I wanted to receive from the Lord. Not being a bashful sort of person, I blurted out, "What you have been preaching about all night!"

Wanting to be exactly sure what this Methodist was requesting from God, Rev. Abrams asked me if I were talking about the Holy Ghost.

"Yes," I replied. "If this is really real and if we can receive this for today, that's what I want from the Lord!"

Rev. Abrams laid his hands on my head and said something about receiving the Holy Spirit. Then the almighty power of the Holy Ghost hit me, and I fell to the floor. I had no catcher then, and for two hours,

I laid on the floor, slain in the Spirit of the Holy Ghost. There truly is an infilling of the Holy Ghost from God for the believer today, and everything is done in God's order. There was nothing spooky or flakey about this experience, but there was the sweetest, warmest filling that began dwelling in my soul in the personage of the Third Person of the Trinity. His mission is to reside in you so He can teach you, lead you, and guide you in your life's journey. Think of it as an extra bonus of power and wisdom.

When Jesus left the earth to return to heaven, He told the disciples He would send the Comforter (John 14). He gave them a command to go out and heal the sick, cast out devils, and preach the Gospel (Mark 15). But His last command to the disciples was for them to return to the Upper Room and wait for the power from on high to be sent down to them (Acts 1). On that day of Pentecost, where 120 people had gathered, the Comforter blew in that room like a mighty wind and filled the whole house first and then all the people who were in the house. The Comforter brought with Him cloven tongues of fire that sat upon each of those gathered, and they began to speak in a language they had not been taught. When this event took place, the noise of the praying and singing caused a stir outside, and other people began coming to the place to see what was happening (Acts 2).

The Bible tells us, in Acts 2, there were approximately 15 different languages spoken in Jerusalem at this time, and as the crowd began to gather around the Upper Room, where the Holy Spirit had descended, each nationality heard its own particular tongue spoken in song and praise to God. How could this be as these disciples and workers had never been taught their languages? Some critics said these disciples and workers were drunk, but Peter, the ignorant and unlearned fisherman, rose to his feet and told them, "This is that which Joel the prophet had prophesied would happen." Because of this testimony of the Holy Spirit, over 3,000 souls were added to the church that day. Two thousand years later, the infilling of the Holy Spirit is still happening to those who seek and desire it. We don't have to wait for it to come to us; we can pray anytime we want for it to come into our spirit.

On the night I received the Holy Spirit, whether I was in my body or out, I really don't know. I just know that when I woke up two hours later lying on the floor over by the organ, I said to myself, "This is the real thing!" Immediately, I thought about the skeptical conversations Joyce and I had earlier about the Holy Spirit. I wondered what she was going to think of my being filled with the Holy Spirit. How in the world could I explain to her about what happened to me when I couldn't understand it all myself?

I got up from the floor and began looking for Joyce among all those still left praying at the altar. When I found her, she was lying on the floor at the other side of the altar, still under the power of the Holy Spirit. She, too, had received the baptism of the Holy Spirit! I wish I could explain exactly how it worked, but I can't. I just chose to believe God's Word, and by accepting it, I allowed God's power to flow through me in any way He chose.

Our experiences of the infilling of the Holy Spirit changed our lives in many ways. Spiritually, we were more alive than ever before and more in tune with the Spirit of Christ. There was more power in our commitment to God and to our work. It was not anything I could point out physically; it was just there. I was teaching Sunday School at this time, leading the singing and anything else I was asked to do. I was so full of the Holy Spirit that it did not make any difference to me what I did just as long as I could praise the Lord by doing it.

Chapter 6

God is Calling Us to Haiti (No, No, No!)

No discipline seems pleasant at the time, but painful. Later on, however, it produces a harvest of righteousness and peace for those who have been trained by it. Hebrews 12:11 (NIV)

ROM MY EXPERIENCE, it seems God likes to speak to his children in the quiet of the night or in the wee hours of the mornings. Perhaps it is at this time He knows we will be listening and not be distracted by the events happening during daytime. It was on such a night at FMC, when I was under one of those 113 personnel carriers installing an inspection plate and thinking about the goodness of God, when suddenly, I heard what seemed like an audible voice say, "I want you to go to Haiti." I came out from under the vehicle, stood up, and looked around to see who had spoken those words. There was no one there. Odd, I thought, I was certain I had heard someone say out loud, "I want you to go to Haiti."

For days, that voice and those words stayed in my heart. I could not get them out of my mind. This command was not to go to some obscure mission field to be determined at a later date, but it was a direct call with a specific place—Haiti. At that time, I knew nothing about Haiti, and I can assure you I had no thoughts ever of becoming a missionary. My total experience with missionaries had not been exactly a pleasant one. Every time missionaries came through our area, they did not seem to have any joy, and they always had these long, sad faces and hard-luck stories to tell the congregations. And besides that cheery note, they were always asking for money for some unknown cause and some unknown individuals I would never know.

Haiti? Where was Haiti anyway? Thinking back, I remembered this older couple who had come to our church whom I believe were missionaries to Haiti, but I couldn't think of anything they ever said or did that made an impression on me or created an interest in my going there. The one thing I knew for certain was I did *not* want to be a missionary to Haiti or to any other place! I simply thought I must be imagining things; give it time, and this notion will go away. But, regardless of how hard I tried, I could not forget the voice that had said, "I want you to go to Haiti."

For the next three years, in the strangest places and strangest times, I continued to hear that voice and those words. I kept trying to ignore them, but during this period, I came to the full realization that the voice I had heard under the personnel carrier was God's. He was calling me to Haiti. It was not a call I wanted, so I ran in the opposite direction as hard and fast as I could.

I stayed busy at the New Queen Shoals Tabernacle, where my father was pastor. Dad had converted one of his mine properties into a church, and he became the pastor. I was doing everything and anything in the church trying to appease God by my good acts. I could not tell Joyce about the call I had received. To say the words out loud would be to acknowledge them, and then I would have to do something about it. Dad sensed something going on in my spirit, but I never told him about the call I had received. Dad was not only my dad but my pastor too, and he knew God was dealing with me in some area of my life. Dad never pried or interfered since he always thought the best thing for me was to let God do the talking.

Once again I found myself worrying about job security. FMC was downsizing, and every week hundreds of employees were being laid off. Joyce and I talked about going to Virginia, where my brother, Buck, was living and working, and starting our own construction company. Looking back on that time, I can see I was trying to get away from the voice that was calling me to Haiti. It had been haunting me steadily for the past three years, and no matter how hard I kept ignoring it and trying to forget that night in the personnel carrier, the voice wouldn't go away. I would try to cast it off by staying busy doing something else for the Lord, trying to make Him happy so He would forget about trying to make me do something I did not want to do. But, I was truly miserable—miserable clear through my skin and into my bones. I began asking some of the same questions King David asked himself:

> "Where can I go from your Spirit? Where can I flee from your presence? If I say, 'Surely the darkness will hide me and the light become night around me? Even the darkness will not be dark to you; the night will shine like the day for darkness is as light to you" (Psalm 139:7, 11-12, NIV).

There was nowhere I could hide from that voice calling me. God's Spirit and His calling were always present. But I kept telling God I did not want to go. Didn't He know that I was not equipped to carry out such a mission? I made it through high school, but I had no college or Bible school. Didn't God know I did not know the first thing about being a missionary?

In the latter part of 1969, Joyce and I made the decision to move to Alexandria, Virginia. Dad went with us, and he and I started a construction business. We attended that "holy roller" church of Buck's, Reality Gospel Church, and we found out they, like we Methodists, enjoyed having revivals.

In January 1970, Evangelist Gene Param from High Point, North Carolina, held a revival at our church. Every night, Rev. Param gave an altar call for those who wanted salvation or any other gift from the Lord. But one particular night, instead of inviting people up to the altar to pray, Rev. Param called three people out of the congregation to come down to the altar. I was one of them. I reached for Joyce's hand, and we headed for the altar. It seemed Rev. Param had some information he had been given from God that he wanted to impart to the three of us.

"Brother Hanson," Rev. Param said, as he leaned over and quietly spoke to me as I was standing there at the altar, "you've been neglecting a call God has placed on your life."

Whoa! A bombshell just landed! Trying to recover from this delightful and surprising message, I acted innocent and said to him, "I believe you are missing the message God is telling you or else you have me mixed up with someone else!"

Without hesitating, Rev. Param said a bit louder, "I'm not missing it, and I know exactly where it is coming from and who it is for!"

I backed away from Param; I did not want to hear this; I did not want to go to Haiti! But deep in my heart, I knew Brother Param had hit the nail on the head, and my head was spinning! Now, my calling was out in the open; it had been spoken audibly. What was I going to do about it?

Typically, when God has established a calling on your life, there comes a decision-making point when you can either: (1) dig your feet in and refuse; or (2) submit. I knew this was my decision-making time! If I dug my feet in and refused, God would probably stop calling me. But if I submitted to that call, I could fall on my face at an altar and tell the Lord I'll do it but only on certain conditions! And the latter is what I did. I spelled it out to God clearly, without any reservations, that my condition was this: If this is what *You* want for our lives then *You* are going to have to tell Joyce! There was no way I was going to tell Joyce she had to become a missionary just because I had a calling on my life. I had been around ministers and their wives all my life. And sometimes I saw pastors carrying on their ministry without any support from their wives. It was a lonely, hard life for a pastor who didn't have his wife's support. I didn't want that in my marriage. If we cannot do it together, it is just not going to happen, Lord. You bet ya! I thought this tough "conditional clause" would surely release me from the calling and get God off my back.

It was pretty quiet in the car on the way home from church that night. I knew Joyce had heard what Rev Param had told me since she was with me at the altar. Also, she had heard my denial. What in the world was she thinking now?

After we put the girls to bed, we lay there beside one another and began talking freely and openly to each other for the first time since I had received the calling. I explained to her about the call I had received from God three years ago when I was under the personnel carrier at FMC. I said that God had called me to go to Haiti. I told her I had been running from that call ever since. I confessed that I had done absolutely nothing about the call; I hadn't even tried to find out anything about Haiti, because I didn't want to go to Haiti.

Next—holding my breath—I told her I had finally submitted to God's calling tonight even though I still didn't want to go to Haiti. At that moment, Joyce began sobbing, louder and louder. "Oh dear," I thought, "she doesn't want to do this either!"

When the tears subsided, Joyce said, "Oh, John, God showed me a vision about Haiti the night I received the Holy Ghost at your dad's church in Queen Shoals, and He gave me another vision about the same time He called you. He confirmed the message in both visions again tonight through Rev Param, but I was too afraid to tell you or anyone."

"Wow," I thought! God had already met my condition before I had even asked, and I was not off the hook! Now that everything was out in the open, we both felt as though a large burden had been lifted from our shoulders. But I wanted to hear more about these visions God had given to Joyce. Joyce was only too happy to tell me about those special times which she calls her "meeting places between God and me."

"My first vision," Joyce began, "came the night I received the baptism in the Holy Spirit at the old Queen Shoals Tabernacle. While I was lying on the floor, not awake, God showed me a vision. When God gives you a vision, it is an imprint on your mind forever!

"Picture an endless cotton field that stretches as far as the eye can see, and it is ready for the harvesters. The green leaves have withered, and all that is left is the snow-white bolls of cotton sitting in the pods on the end of the brown prickly stems. At a distance, the field appears to be totally white. As I draw closer to the plants, I see that each plant is laboring under its load of white bolls. It is quite obvious that the ladened down plant needs to be harvested. I was familiar with the scripture in St. John where Jesus tells the people to, '*Open your eyes and look at the fields! They are ripe for harvest. Even now the reaper draws his wages, even now he harvests the crop for eternal life, so that the sower and the reaper may be glad together*' (John 4:35, NIV). I knew without any doubt God was calling me to be a harvester. And I knew being a harvester meant He was calling me to be a missionary to tell others about Christ's plan of salvation and bring them into His eternal storehouse.

"When I awoke from being 'slain in the spirit,' as some refer to it, the vision was still fresh on my mind. But I had just been filled with the Holy Spirit, and I was bubbling over with joy as I was speaking in a language I had never learned and did not know. I was completely awed by this experience. It took me about two days before I could open my mouth and speak English, because the Holy Spirit had consumed me. I pushed the vision to the back of my mind as the days went by.

The Bible says that if we hunger and thirst after righteousness, we shall be filled, and I was filled to overflowing on that night.

"I didn't share this vision with you, John, because I didn't know if He was calling you too. I kept it to myself. Later on, God showed me another vision similar to the first one while I was at the altar one evening at Reality Gospel Church. Sometimes when God gives you a vision, He will also give you another one just to confirm the original one. If you have any doubts, God wants to clear them up.

"My second vision was different from the first one in that I was in the same white field, but I was walking through the field carrying a basket on my arm. The bolls were still heavy on the pods, and I saw myself bending down picking off a boll. As I put the boll into my basket, that boll turned into a beautiful brown face. I picked another boll, and before it reached my basket, it turned into another brown, smiling face staring up at me. This happened each time I picked a boll from the plant. Realizing I was harvesting people, I began frantically trying to pick all the cotton bolls and put them into my basket. I became discouraged quickly, because there were too many bolls, too many brown faces. I knew the Scriptures said, *'The harvest is plentiful but the workers are few.'* The field was too large, and there were not enough workers to pick all the bolls. God made me aware that the crop would wither and die on the plant if I did not pick all the bolls. I knew if I did not harvest the people, they would perish without knowing God.

"It was so clear to me that God was telling me there are souls in Haiti waiting to be taught His plan of salvation, and He is holding me accountable for them. It was a terribly awesome and terrifying commission. I knew that God wanted this harvest completed, and He was calling me to do it.

"And tonight, John, as I stood beside you and heard Rev Param telling you that God was showing him how you were not responding to your call, I knew that was my third confirmation that I was to be a missionary, for I knew you had the calling too."

When Joyce finished telling me about her visions, I was awed by God's divine calling and how He had confirmed it with Joyce not once but three times. It was amazing how His voice had dealt with my spirit again and again and had not given up on us. We prayed together and confessed we did not know exactly what God had in store for us, but whatever it was, we were now willing to go where He wanted us to and do what He wanted us to do—even if it was to the middle of the Caribbean Ocean in a small country called Haiti. Finally, Joyce and I were in the same hymnal, on the same page, singing the same song!

CHAPTER 7

Answering the Call (Almost)

*. . . The harvest is plentiful but the workers
are few. Matthew 9:37 (NIV)*

WHEN YOU RUN from a calling God has placed on your life, you cannot possess the peace that surpasses all understanding. In fact, it is really hard to possess any kind of peace at all. Mostly, you are more miserable than not. It is unsettling being in a constant state of questioning everything you do. You wonder if what you are doing for God will be "good" enough, while all the time, you know in your heart it is not exactly what He has called you to do. When I had enough of the misery and finally submitted to God's calling, the peace that came through my total surrender was very sweet.

Unfortunately, the sweetness lasted but for a short period before the questions and uncertainties began to fill my mind. For certain questions, I knew the answers—like, *where* was I to go? Haiti, of course. *What* was I supposed to do? Preach the Gospel, naturally.

Who was I to preach to? The people of Haiti. But **when** I was to go and **how** was I going to do it? Well, I did not have a clue!

After our confessions to one another of the callings God placed on our lives, Joyce and I continued our church activities, doing what we had been doing for years and waiting for a few suggestions from God. I would fill in for leading the praise and worship service, we both taught Sunday School, and we did anything and everything anyone asked us to do. We did all this while waiting, praying, and fasting for further instructions from God. Meanwhile, I told Dad about my calling, as well as all the questions I had that needed answers. What I wanted, I told him, was to find a place to start.

In June 1969, Dad had a good idea. He was going to make contact with the older missionary couple to Haiti who visited our church yearly and were supported by the Gospel Tabernacle denomination. When Dad talked with the missionaries, he told them of God's calling on our lives and our desire to become missionaries to Haiti. I thought this just might lead to an open door for us.

This older couple, who had been life-long missionaries to Haiti, told us they were excited about the possibility of our becoming missionaries. They gave us all the information and forms needed to apply to the Gospel Tabernacle Conference for missionary status to Haiti. Joyce and I completed the numerous forms required and listed our qualifications, which were skimpy at best. We wrote our testimony about how God had called us to go to Haiti after we had received the baptism of the Holy Ghost. Anxiously, we returned the completed forms to our missionary friends.

A few days passed, and we began to see a change in this couple's enthusiasm toward us regarding our desire to go to Haiti. Earlier, they had been thrilled and anxious for us to join them; now, they seemed apprehensive and evasive when answering our questions as to when and how we would begin. After several puzzling phone conversations, they told us we would have to appear before the Gospel Tabernacle Conference Board to be approved and ordained before we could be assigned to Haiti. This seemed reasonable, so we prepared to move on to this next step.

My brother, Buck, who by this time was an evangelist, had expressed a desire to become ordained in the Gospel Tabernacle Conference. So, he, too, filled out all the necessary paperwork. We both looked forward to appearing before the board to receive our ordination papers.

On the day of our ordination, Buck and I stood with high expectations before a board of men who had known us all our lives. We were very familiar with the board members, because Dad had worked with them on church projects and had preached in revivals all his life. These men knew our characters, and they knew our record of Christian service and faithfulness to God. As Buck and I stood before these men, anxiously wanting to join their organization, the board sadly told us they could not ordain us into their denomination. The reason the board gave for not ordaining us was that we confessed to having been filled with the baptism of the Holy Ghost and having spoken in tongues. They explained to us that they did not believe in the baptism of the Holy Ghost nor did they believe in speaking in tongues.

Needless to say, neither Buck nor I would deny what God had done in our lives through the Holy Spirit, even if it meant we would be rejected for ordination, and I would not get to go to Haiti. We were shocked and disappointed, but mostly, we were hurt that our rejection was because of the infilling of the Holy Spirit in our lives. My mind kept thinking about the scripture verse in Amos which says, "Do two walk together unless they have agreed to do so?" (Amos 3:3, NIV). I knew if that leadership and I didn't agree on the infilling of the precious Holy Spirit, then it was best that Joyce and I not pursue going to Haiti with them or *anyone* who did not believe in the baptism of the Holy Spirit.

It was good that we discovered in the beginning how the Gospel Tabernacle Conference believed, because our association with them would have never worked. But even with this knowledge, it did not stop the disappointment from flooding our minds and spirits. We also realized that when our missionary friends had read our application forms, they understood that we would never be ordained in their conference because of our confession of the baptism of the Holy Ghost. While the man was a member of the Conference Board, neither he nor his wife had the courage to give us this information; they preferred to let the board do it. The board's rejection was like a door being slammed shut in my face!

For the next six years, Joyce and I continued to work in our church and wait for God to reveal to us the next step. Waiting is a hard task. How many times did I ask myself, "Did God really tell me to go to Haiti?" And the answer was always the same—an emphatic "Yes!" Then, why wasn't God telling us or sending someone to tell us what to do next? What was I supposed to do? Was God testing my patience, or was He testing my creativeness to see if I could come up with a plan? I was not interested in any counterfeit plan; I wanted God's plan for our lives, and only God's. It seemed like an eternity waiting without any answers to my questions. All Joyce and I could do was to keep putting our trust fully in the One who had called us to Haiti.

In February 1970, Evangelist Harold Atkins, from Hendersonville, North Carolina, held a seven-night revival in our Pentecostal Reality Church in Alexandria, Virginia. While Harold was in town, my Dad and I enjoyed visiting with him several times. One evening during our fellowship time, Harold told me he was going to Haiti to a Christian Haitian Conference the end of February. And guess what? He wanted me to go with him! I knew this was another door opening for me, and I could see the light bursting through. After all the years of waiting, I wanted to walk through that door. I was anxious as a child on Christmas Day to walk through that open door to Haiti. After my experience in with Evangelist Param, who had confronted me about not answering my call, I was saying a big "YES" to anything that had to do with God calling me to Haiti. It was amazing to see how God could take such a closed mind as mine and open it to *any* and *all* things He had planned for me.

It is important to understand here that Joyce and I had no instruction manual from God explaining step-by-step how He was going to use us as missionaries to Haiti. Without any hesitations or doubts, all we knew for sure was that God had called us to minister to the people of Haiti. Since we had been praying diligently for God to show us how He was to use us, this trip with Rev. Atkins seemed to be an answer to our prayers. After discussing it with Joyce, we agreed that I would make the first trip, and Joyce would stay home with the girls. By this time, I had seen a few slides and heard a few stories about Haiti, and I wanted first to see for myself what God had in store for us in that exciting country. You might say that I wanted to test the waters before I committed my family to anything long term.

Finally, when the day came to leave for Haiti, I could hardly contain my excitement. As Rev. Harold Atkins, his brother, Rev. Larry Atkins, and I boarded the huge Pan Am airplane at Miami International Airport, it was exhilarating to be making my first trip to Haiti to a Christian Haitian Conference.

In only a few hours, we were landing on a small airport runway in Port-au-Prince, where all I could see were fields of crude huts and brown-skinned Haitians. My heart began pumping so fast I thought it might jump out of my body! At last, I was here in Haiti—the place God had called me to minister to His people. I was thrilled to be stepping out of the plane onto Haitian ground, surrounded by mountains in the distance.

Mountains? I had expected an island to be flat all over. Mountains were good; as a matter of fact, mountains were great! It felt as though I were coming home. I fell in love with the country and the people immediately. They were such a friendly and gracious group. Amazingly, God had tucked that love away in my heart when He called me to go to Haiti, and I wasn't even aware that He had put it there. Now it was coming out in full force, and it swelled up in me like the hot rays of sunshine that shone down on Haiti. These were my people; I was given the awesome task of being their pastor, leading them to eternal life. This first trip was the beginning of my six-year relationship with the people of Haiti as a non-resident missionary.

A Haitian pastor, who Rev. Atkins knew, met us at the airport and was our guide and interpreter for the duration of the week-long trip. Rev. Atkins had met this pastor on one of his previous trips to Haiti, and he wanted to introduce him to me. We were taken out to Petit Goâve, a rural area, far away from the city of Port-au-Prince. Here was a large church set up for the convention services, with benches that looked like they could fall apart at any time. It seemed that this Haitian pastor worked with many of the local churches, and every year in February, they invited pastors from all over the United States to come to their convention. This was a way for the Haitian pastors to garner financial support from pastors in the United States.

One day during my first Haitian convention, I was walking around taking a break in between services and soaking up the local atmosphere. I spotted an old woman cooking rice in a smoke-filled hut. There were about 1,500 people at this convention that needed to be fed, and this lady was one of the women hired to cook for the attendees. She had on a raggedy old dress torn in several places, with no shoes on her feet and no teeth in her mouth. I learned later she was only 40 years old at that time, but those years had not been kind to her. This lady had six children whom she was raising all by herself. That is enough to make anyone look old! She smiled at me, and I smiled back, noticing that her hands looked as though they had been scraped with a tin cabbage grater. They were red and raw and looked as though something had eaten the skin away. I could only imagine how much pain this condition caused her. She introduced herself as Madam Andre. Being filled with compassion for this poor unfortunate woman, I took her hands in mine and prayed for her. Later, I thought maybe I shouldn't have held her hands like I did;

she might have had some contagious disease and passed it on to me. But at that time, all I wanted to do was to let her know that I cared and God did too. After the prayer, I moved on, and Madam Andre thanked me graciously.

Skipping a little ahead to my second visit to the Haitian Convention, in the same place at Petit-Goâve, someone came up to me and gave me a big hug. I looked down and discovered it was Madam Andre. She was smiling and so happy to see me. It was then she told me that after I had prayed for her, God had healed her hands! I looked at her hands, expecting to see them red and raw as they once had been. Instead, I saw a new pair of hands, healthy and clean. She also told me that God had spoken to her at the time her hands were healed and told her that one day she would work for me.

One day several years later, when we moved to Haiti permanently, Madam Andre showed up on our doorstep. Eventually, Madam Andre became the head cook at our Bible school and was like a second mother to our two daughters, Cindy and Faithe. Madam Andre loved to pray, and she knew how to touch heaven when she prayed. What a blessing it was to have her in our presence every day. Many years later when she was near death, she asked us to take her back home to Petit-Goâve to die. On a Wednesday, we took her home and said we would be back to see her Sunday afternoon after church. But, Wednesday was the last time we saw her alive. She died that same night around 10:30 p.m. in her home with her family. How wonderful it is when God places such loving people in your life to encourage and strengthen you.

Getting back to my first visit to the Haitian Convention, we American pastors attended church services every night. During the daytime, we were taken on visits to churches in the Petit-Goâve area and then driven to the far out boonies to see the brush arbor churches. The most sobering trip was to the orphanage at Petit-Goâve. There just isn't anything that touches a person's heart like that of a child who is neglected, alone, and hungry. We were seeing many children who had no homes and nothing to eat until they came to this orphanage. At this time, I could not speak the Creole language, but the language barrier did not keep me from seeing the poverty that existed in this orphanage and everywhere else in this land. Every pastor, whose heart was touched by these orphans, pledged to do his best to send support for these children.

Every convention began on Tuesday and ran through the following Sunday, ending with a baptismal service in the ocean at Petit-Goâve. All the American pastors were invited to stay and participate in the Sunday baptismal service. Sometimes there would be as many as seven or eight pastors baptizing over 300 converts in the ocean. During one baptismal service, several young and playful boys were jumping in and out of their canoes, naked as jaybirds, doing their best to interrupt the service. Several people threw rocks at them and tried to shoo them away, but to no avail. It really was one funny riot. The pastors managed to get all the new converts baptized, but it was a circus seeing all the people trying to curtail those young boys bent on their mischief.

After my first convention, I returned home with lots of stories to tell Joyce and the girls. I told her how much I felt at home in Haiti with the people. It sure was great to return to my nice, soft bed in my cool, air-conditioned home, after a week of sleeping on a hard army cot and sweating in the humid heat.

My heart had been touched deeply by everything I had seen in Haiti. However, I kept telling myself that I could do so much more by staying here in the United States and earning the money for supplies to be sent to the people of Haiti. And this was the beginning of my six-year campaign of reasoning and bargaining with the Lord, trying to convince Him that my way was better.

CHAPTER 8

Submission to the Call

*. . . I tell you, open your eyes and look at the fields!
They are ripe for harvest. John 4:35 (NIV)*

ON AUGUST 1970, I made my second trip to Haiti. This time Joyce went with me. Like me, Joyce fell in love with the people and was thrilled to be there at last. She had agonized for so many years over her calling, and finally, she was where she knew God wanted her to be.

We had been so touched by the orphaned children that we wanted to start our own orphanage to help take care of the homeless children and to provide food and an education for them. The same Haitian pastor, who I had met on my first trip to Haiti, told us of a place in the town of Léogâne where there was a building we could rent that would be suitable for an orphanage. And thus began a small orphanage housing 32 children, two teachers, and a cook. Our pastor friend would give leadership, and we pledged to help him all we could.

When we returned home, we began sending money to this

local pastor and his organization for support of this orphanage. For governmental reasons, we set up the orphanage in the name of the organization we would be ministering under in Haiti. We called the orphanage *Love Missions Outreach*. We thought it was an appropriate name since we were reaching out to these children through the love of Jesus.

Thereafter, Joyce and I made two trips every year—one in February to attend the Haitian Convention and one in the fall to minister to the people. Every trip to Haiti brought us closer and closer to the people. Every year, God showed us something else we needed to be doing for the Haitians. Sometimes, we took other pastors or lay people with us, and sometimes we went alone. After each trip, we saw our love for the Haitians grow. We also saw more needs for the Haitian people, so we branched out and began sending money to the Haitian pastor to build new churches.

In the six years between my first trip to Haiti and the time we arrived there to live permanently, we helped build eight churches along with contributing to our orphanage. We also bought two vehicles, a Chevrolet Suburban and a Jeep. Joyce and the girls collected food, clothing, medical supplies, and other items from everyone and everywhere for the people of the poverty-stricken country. Many days we could hardly walk through our home because of the stacked up boxes waiting to be taken to Haiti when we made our bi-annual trips. We put as much stuff in our luggage as we could and boxed up the other items. On some trips, we took teens to visit and work in the Haitian churches. However, we felt our girls were too young to make the trip, so they never saw Haiti until we moved there permanently.

During those six years of traveling back and forth to Haiti, our construction business in Alexandria, Virginia, grew more and more successful. We experienced many difficulties while starting our construction business, but each problem became another way we learned perseverance and patience in getting to the place where God wanted us to go. The construction business was just another training ground God provided for us to learn to live by faith and not by sight.

I became the assistant pastor at Pentecostal Reality Church in Alexandria, Virginia, and Brother Cox, the pastor, became not only my pastor but a dearly beloved friend. We went through the construction of a new worship center, and I, along with many other men in the church, supervised and financially supported the new church building. Sometimes, I would lead the praise and worship service. As our construction business grew, we tried even harder to help provide for the ever-growing needs of our friends and co-workers in Christ in Haiti.

We were working in our church every spare moment available, and our construction business took up the rest of our time. A lot of the money we made went to support the projects in Haiti. Of course, these offerings were given after we first paid our tithes to our local church. I believe strongly in the scripture in Malachi, chapter 3, which says to bring the tithe into the storehouse first so as not to rob God. I am persuaded that this is the reason God has blessed Joyce and me so much. And God did, indeed, bless us in our construction business. I did not hesitate to use this often as a point of reasoning with God. My reasoning with God went something like this:

> *"Surely, God, I can accomplish much more by staying here and earning a profitable living than I could ever do by going and living in Haiti. Don't you see all the wonderful deeds we are doing with the money we are earning here, and I am sure you must be pleased with all our gifts?"*

But God's answer to all my sound reasoning was the same every time: "I TOLD YOU TO *GO* TO HAITI!"

The last time God said, "I told you to go to Haiti" was the last time He had to tell me. Somehow, after six years of trying to appease God with our good works, Joyce and I knew it was time to put up or shut up. We decided to "put up," and literally, we put everything we had on the line. We told our families and friends, our pastor and church family, and everyone we knew that we were moving to Haiti. We actually expected everyone to be as excited about it as we were. However, we found that most of them thought we had lost our senses. Some people even told us they definitely thought we were missing the will of God. If one of my friends had told me he was taking his family and moving to a foreign land where he did not have a job or any means of support and could not even speak the language, I probably would have felt he was a little crazy too.

To move out in faith and do something as impractical as what we were planning, you have to "know that you know, that you know that you know" you are in the will of God! Joyce and I had talked it over numerous times, and we both knew it was time to go to Haiti. We discussed the primitiveness of the country and how remote it would be from family and friends. We also talked about "if" or "how" our girls would adjust to these circumstances. Joyce knew she would be isolated from all she had ever known in her life. As a mother, it would hurt Joyce most of all to take her girls away from their friends and loved ones, yanking them out of their comfort zone. But like me, Joyce had God's calling burned into her spirit, and nothing less than moving to Haiti was going to give her peace with her calling. God had entrusted us with an awesome responsibility. God would surely hold us accountable for the lost souls in Haiti He had assigned us to if we did not go to Haiti. That accountability weighed heavily on our hearts.

We were going to Haiti, and that was final! My dear Pastor Cox was devastated when I told him we were leaving. He told me we had accomplished a great deal together these past few years, and he knew it had been God's will for me to be his assistant pastor. Pastor Cox tried to reason with me. He said I needed to think and pray more about this before I did something so drastic as to close my business and take my family off to a foreign land with no support or guarantees of help from anyone or any organization. He told me we needed to attend at least a two-year Bible school where we could get training on how to teach the God's Word to the Haitians and how to be missionaries.

It was truly disheartening not getting the blessings of Pastor Cox and the church on our decision to move to Haiti. That day we left for Haiti, besides our family, only four friends came to see us off at the airport. I put up a strong front and kept smiling as they all wished us well and said their goodbyes. Heavy as our hearts were, I thanked God for the wonderful peace He gave me that surpassed all of man's understanding of our decision. I had chosen to find favor with God instead of man, but boy, did it hurt!

I discovered later that Pastor Cox's reasoning regarding training had definitely been sound advice, for spending a couple of years in a Bible school prior to leaving would have been tremendously helpful to us. But in my enthusiasm and ignorance, I could not see it then. There are times when you need to listen to the voice of reason. If I had just listened to Pastor Cox's wisdom and attended a Bible school, I could have been saved from making a lot of mistakes in the beginning. I knew nothing about how missionaries did things, such as raising funds, starting churches, and gathering support. I had been fed on the Word of God all my life, and I thought I knew how to preach it. I thought that was all I needed to know.

For the past six years, I had heard God's voice telling me to go to Haiti, and I had made up my mind that His was the only voice I was going to listen to concerning this move. No one could really know how tired I was of trying to bargain with that voice. And when my bargaining did not work, I kept running from that voice. I was sick and tired of running! At that time, I was ready *"right now"* to do exactly what that voice was telling me to do.

CHAPTER 9

Moving to Haiti

*"Do not be deceived: God cannot be mocked. A man
reaps what he sows. Galatians 6:7 (NIV)*

SITTING IN THE crowded Pan Am jet's coach class on our way
to Haiti with Joyce, the girls, and Faithe's three-year-old black
poodle, Princess, I thought about the past few months of our lives.
What a whirlwind it had been for this year, 1976! Shutting down our
construction business and selling off all the equipment was difficult,
but selling all our personal possessions—that was truly emotional
and draining.

Joyce and the girls were real troopers, culling out the items we
could actually take with us to Haiti from the ones we had to sell or
give away. We narrowed down our possessions to a few personal items
and some clothing that we put in a couple of old trunks. Then we
decided to take a small gas kitchen stove for cooking, a small electric
refrigerator, a round green card table with four chairs, and a small
black and white TV.

All these items were loaded in a 1972 Ford pickup truck that we would use in Haiti for travel. That Ford truck, with all of our worldly possessions, was now on a boat to Haiti, and we could only hope it got there shortly after we arrived. It was all a pretty meager lot considering the abundance of provisions God had blessed us with in the past 16 years of marriage.

We all cried as we hugged the family members and friends who had come to see us off at Reagan Airport in Arlington, Virginia. We knew we were going to miss all these people who were a part of our daily lives. Princess was barking her head off, and I didn't know if it was because she did not want to go or because she was excited about going. When we had given Princess to Faithe as a birthday present, she was only a puppy, so we could not bear to part with her.

Amid all the crying and barking, we managed to board the plane and get ourselves settled. I kept thinking about what my family and friends were thinking about right now. I knew some of them thought I had lost my mind making this move with my family. But others knew how strong my conviction was in answering God's calling on my life, and I like to think they understood a little bit of why I had to do this. The few church members who came were people we saw every week and ate out with after church. After working all day at our regular jobs, we had spent many evenings with these friends working together on the construction of our new church auditorium. We had helped increased our church membership together, starting with about a hundred members which now totaled between 600 and 700 every Sunday morning for two services. Yes, we would certainly miss the fellowship of all these friends and family.

Now, we were on our way. It had been very important to me that we have a home waiting for us when we arrived in Haiti, so the Haitian pastor, whom Rev. Atkins had introduced to me on my first visit to Haiti, rented a small place for us in La Boule, which was about 15 miles outside of Port-au-Prince. I was able to pay rent two months in advance. I knew Joyce and the girls were sacrificing so many things as it was, and I couldn't stand the thought of my family not knowing whether or not they were going to have a roof over their heads.

When we moved to Haiti, Cindy was 15 years old and only had two years left of high school, and Faithe was 11 years old. Even though the girls were giving up their friends and most of their treasured possessions, they optimistically looked upon this as a big adventure. For the past six years, they had been such a big part of collecting food, clothing, and school supplies for the Haitians that I believe they were really excited about finally getting to see the country they had heard so much about. I knew they would miss the comfort of their home and miss their friends, but this was a big opportunity to live and learn in another country. This was something that most teenagers would never have a chance to do. I believed the girls would do just fine.

When we landed at the airport in Port-au-Prince, it felt different this time. This was not just an annual visit to the Haitian Convention with side trips to an outstation and a quick exit back to my comfortable home. Now, we were here to live!

The Haitian pastor met us at the airport in Port-au-Prince and said we could stay with him for a few days until our Ford pickup cleared customs. Even though we had rented a house, it had no furniture or stove or anything that would enable us to stay there. It was a pretty nice house, about 1,200 square feet in space, with three bedrooms and two bathrooms. The house was located at the end of a road on a hillside in La Boule. From the front and backyard, we had a beautiful view of the hills that surrounded our small town. By American standards, it wasn't fancy, but to us, it quickly became our home sweet home.

It took a couple of weeks before our Ford cleared customs, and we were able to move into our new home. "Move" is a general term for what we did, but actually, all we had to move were the mattresses the

Haitian pastor had loaned us to sleep on and our meager possessions from the Ford truck. We put the small gas stove in the kitchen and the card table with the four chairs in our dining room. The card table and chairs served as a place to eat, as well as furniture to sit upon in our living room.

I remember the day we got that green card table; we had used the yellow Top Value stamps that Piggly Wiggly grocery stores used to give away. Back then all grocery stores had some type of gimmick to get you to buy from them. Piggly Wiggly gave customers one stamp for every one-dollar's worth of groceries purchased. You licked that stamp and put it in a small booklet, and when you had filled that booklet, you could redeem it for gifts at one of the gift redemption centers. Of course, the more books you had filled with stamps, the more expensive item you could purchase. I had no idea at that time how valuable that *free* card table would become in our new home in Haiti!

After we emptied our personal items and clothing from the trunks, we used the two trunks in the living room as a coffee and an end table to compliment our card table chairs. And that was pretty much our "moving in." Without many furnishings, our small, but nice, home looked pretty large to us. We had electricity, but it was not very dependable. Blackouts were common and still are to this day. If we could have afforded it, a generator would have kept us from spending lots of time in the dark. But it was another ten years before our budget would include a major item like a generator. We had no way to heat the house, but thankfully, we rarely needed heat in such a warm climate as Haiti.

The small black and white TV was useless since there was no service available, so it rested in a closet for many years. There was no telephone service available, and even if there had been, we would not have been able to afford it. The closest phone was in Port-au-Prince; we had to drive 15 miles to use it. It was a big event to make a phone call back to the States. After the drive to

Port-au-Prince to where the building with the public phones was located, our whole family crammed ourselves into a single phone booth. With no air conditioning, not only was it cramped, but it was sweltering hot. One by one we talked with grandparents and other kin, just to hear their voices and let them know we were all still alive. These conditions were how we lived and slept for the first five years we were in Haiti. I did a lot of fasting those first five years!

After selling off all our possessions and paying all our debts, we arrived in Haiti with about $2,200 in our pockets. We had not raised any money to come to Haiti, and we did not have any organization or churches promising support to us. Let me be completely honest here and say *we knew nothing about how missions worked or what you needed to do before going on the mission field!* We had talked with eight individuals who said they would try to send us $10 a month, but to my recollection we never ever saw any of that money. Even if that $80 per month had come in, I must have been pretty naïve to think we could live on that amount per month! In this day and age, it must seem pretty incredible that I could have been so uninformed and ignorant. But, that first year in Haiti, we lived on only $7,200 for the entire year. It was by God's grace that we made it. Back then, though, despite all my inexperience, all I knew was God had told me to go live in Haiti and minister to His people. There is something about a calling from God that when He speaks to you, you know you *must* do what He says.

If Joyce and I had not known for sure beyond any doubt that God had called us to Haiti, we could have jumped off in many a good quitting place!

Cindy and Faithe outside our first home in La Boule, Haiti

CHAPTER 10

Disappointment and Reassurance

. . . Give careful thought to your ways. You have planted much, but have harvested little. Haggai 1:5, 6 (NIV)

I T DID NOT take long for word to get around the neighborhood that we were missionaries, and people began coming to us for help. Words cannot describe the needs we saw. There was hunger everywhere, but there were so many medical needs too. And the greatest need of all was the lack of the Gospel of Jesus Christ being preached to the people. I knew why God had called us to Haiti; these people were desperate for the love of God and His Son, and they did not even know it. Before poverty and sickness can be addressed, or before you can give people assurance that their lives can be better, you have to teach them about the Life Changer. You have to tell them how He wants to change their spiritual life before He can change their physical life. Once you introduce them to the One who gives them eternal life, then physical change is inevitable.

But there is another side too. When bellies are empty, it is hard to convince them that Jesus loves them. They need to *see* the love Jesus has for them, and they need to *see* the love we have for them.

So, little by little each day, we began to share with the people of Haiti our Lord and Savior, Jesus Christ. Sometimes it was on the streets of the city of Port-au-Prince, and sometimes it was in a brush arbor church out in the country where someone wanted our help building a permanent church. It really did not matter where. All that mattered was we were here sharing the Word of God to this nation of people whom God loved enough to call us out of our comfortable life in the United States to minister to them. And along with the sharing of the Word, we shared whatever possessions we had. Sometimes it was food, and sometimes it was medical supplies. Often I shared my knowledge of construction or my auto mechanical knowledge. Sometimes all we shared was a ride into town. As the people began to see that we were willing to share what we had, they began to listen as we shared the Word of God.

The first things Joyce and I wanted to see when we arrived in Haiti were all the churches we had helped build in the far out country regions and our Love Missions Outreach orphanage. Even though we had been coming down here for six years, we had never been to any of those outstation churches we had built and supported. It was not that we hadn't wanted to visit the churches, but each time we asked to see them, the Haitian pastor had some excuse as to why we could not travel on the roads. Sometimes he told us the rains had washed out the roads, and other times he said the churches were closed for some governmental reason.

Now that we were here on a permanent basis, we were anxious to see those eight churches we had built and supported. We kept asking the Haitian pastor to take us to them. After repeated attempts to get him to take us to the churches and receiving different excuses, the Haitian pastor broke down and confessed that not one church had ever been built with our funds! And our orphanage that we had been faithfully supporting every month for the last six years? It was a sham too! How could this be? We had seen the orphanage in the beginning with our own eyes.

"Very easy," the Haitian pastor confessed sheepishly. He said when pastors came through for the Haitian Convention, he and his employees collected children from the neighborhood and took them to an empty building and pretended that it was the beginning of an orphanage. Whatever pastor was being shown the pretend orphanage, the Haitian pastor would put that visiting pastor's sign up in front of the building. When the visiting pastor left town and went back to the States, the sign would come down, and the children would go back home.

This Haitian pastor, the very same person who I had been introduced to on my first trip to Haiti and who had been my friend and source of information these past six years, gave no explanation as to what he had done with the thousands of dollars my family and other church families had given throughout the years. Instead of regretting his actions, he was very angry that we had discovered his deception. We knew he was also a business man owning taxis, cargo trucks and houses, so we could only assume he spent the money increasing his profits on his businesses and on himself. What a racket he had going on! Is there anything more despicable than using starving and unwanted children to solicit money? And we had fallen—hook, line and sinker—for the whole scheme! If we had stayed in the States, we would have continued sending money to him, only to have him use it for his personal gain instead of the Lord's work. Proverbs 14:31 says, "He who oppresses the poor reproaches his Maker . . ." (NKJV).

I cannot stress to you enough how important it is that you know beyond a doubt where your offerings are going!

To say that Joyce and I were devastated—well, "devastated" is a mild term when describing how we felt. Not only had we sent money for eight churches (one which was supposed to have been built as a memorial for Joyce's father who had passed away) and an orphanage, we had bought a Jeep and a Suburban and sent them there for the pastors of two of those churches. In addition, we were still making payments on that Suburban!

When you get your feet knocked out from under you, you usually fall to the ground. I fell good and hard. The air had been knocked out of me when I hit the ground, and all six feet, two inches of me wanted to pound that little man into the ground! The Haitian pastor told us we could have the Suburban back if we paid the duty and taxes on it. We had already paid the duty and taxes once, and I politely told him to keep the Suburban. I told him clearly and without stuttering, "What I gave to God, I don't want back. What you do with it is up to you!" Needless to say, our association with that *pastor* ended that day.

After that ordeal, if (and that's a mighty big IF) we had ever had any doubts at all about our calling to Haiti, we would have packed up and left Haiti for good. Yes, we were angry, hurt, disappointed, and kicking ourselves for being so gullible, but we never doubted our calling. Actually, we were more sure than ever that we were called to minister to and love these precious people who were doing *anything* and *everything* to survive in a country that was the poorest nation in the western hemisphere.

We had been in Haiti a little over two months, and the cash in my wallet had dwindled down to $25. We had shared with the people all we had brought with us, but we had received no money from any sources. I had borrowed from Faithe and Cindy all the money they had saved to come here, and that had hurt my pride deeply. I had promised to repay them, but I didn't know when that would be. It is a very humbling thing for a parent to have to borrow money from their children.

It was on a Friday evening that I had a quiet talk with Joyce after the girls had gone to bed. I had been praying so hard for God to show me what to do, but I wasn't getting any answers from Him.

"I made a decision on my own," I told Joyce. "I am going to send the girls and you home. I can't bear the thought of you all being hungry and trying to tough it out."

I went on to explain to her that we were down to our last $25, and no money had come in since we had been here; I didn't know how we were going to continue to pay rent and put food on the table.

Joyce knew I had spent many days fasting and praying, asking God for His help and guidance. She knew I had not made this decision lightly. Sometimes as I sat outside our house at night looking up into the heavens, I felt like Job wondering where God was in all of this. Why wasn't He giving me some answers? Even though I did not know the answers or what the outcome was going to be, I knew I had to use my faith in my God to bring me through. Sometimes it is just that simple—we have to trust Him. Do you know of a better gift we can give God than our trust?

I firmly believe that this was Satan's biggest attempt to get me to quit and go home. He knew how precious my family was to me, and I would never let them suffer. But what he hadn't counted on was that I was not going home with them! We had our return trip tickets that had been purchased when we came to Haiti, since it was required if you were not a local resident. I explained to Joyce that I could tough it out, but I would not subject her and the girls to the hardships. I knew that back home my family and Joyce's family would make sure they were cared for. And besides, right now we were just floundering around here without contacts with a local organization that could direct us to the needs of the people. The realization of what that Haitian pastor had done caused me to sever ties with his organization immediately, so we really had no "in" with anyone here. But there was no way I could be a part of that man's ministry. The funny thing was, when I told him I would no longer participate in his phony ministry, he came and took back the mattresses we had borrowed from him. Now, our house was barer than ever!

When we woke up Saturday morning, solemnly I outlined for Joyce my plan. "I am going to go down to the post office and ask for our mail. If I don't hear from someone who has sent us some money, I am sending you and the girls back to West Virginia to my mom's and dad's home, as I know you will be all right there. I am going to stay here and see this through, as I know beyond any doubt we have been called by God to minister in Haiti."

I got in my Ford pickup and drove to Port-au-Prince to the post office. Feeling every bump and rut in the road, I knew I was coming closer to carrying out the tough decision I had made the previous night. As I entered the post office, my pulse quickened and my hands shook. I asked for my mail as calmly as I could, and a worker handed me a few envelopes.

"Good," I thought, "there were several envelopes. Maybe, just maybe, there might be some money in one."

I couldn't wait till I got outside, so right there in the middle of the Port-au-Prince post office, I ripped open all the letters. In one envelope, Praise God, there was a check for $800 sent to us by a friend named David Simkins who lived in Virginia. With all the postal workers looking on and probably thinking "that poor missionary has gone plumb crazy," I shouted and praised God for answering my prayers.

I had heard from heaven, loudly and clearly! I was walking on air as I headed outside to go home. As I approached my pickup, I saw the lady we had always bought vegetables from standing there waiting for me. She had put a bushel basket full of different kinds of vegetables in the bed of the truck.

"No, I can't buy today," I politely told her. Yes, I had the miraculous $800 check in my hand, and as soon as I could get to the bank, I would have some cash. But for right now, I did not have a dime in my pocket.

Smiling, she shook her head. "No," she said, "I do not want any money. The vegetables are a gift to you and your family."

Graciously, I thanked her and practically flew down the bumpy road in my pickup to our home. When Joyce saw me run from the truck to the house, she knew she and the girls did not have to go back to West Virginia. We were all so happy that day; we feasted on the basket of vegetables, and the $800 check meant we all got to stay in Haiti together. God is so faithful, and He does all things well. Besides that, His timing is always perfect!

From that day forward, we have never been in that type of situation again. Joyce later confided to me that she had made up her mind that if I made the decision to send them back to West Virginia, she was staying with me. She said she had been called to Haiti too, and she wasn't going home until *God* told her to.

Sometimes it is necessary for you to know for yourself how serious you are about doing God's will. Occasionally, God will let you go through difficulties, just to see if you are able to trust Him in the small things. If you cannot trust Him in the small things, you will never get to experience the greater things He has in store for you. I know I was willing to give up my family, and I know Joyce was willing to give up her children to answer God's calling. God knew all along how serious we were, and now, *we* knew how serious we were!

The kind lady who gave us the vegetables? Well, when she comes to the compound in Delmas, I have instructed the staff to give her anything we have that she needs, whether it is clothing, food, or anything medical. We have even helped her build a small home for her family. You never know the dividends you may reap from one sincere act of kindness!

Haitian lady on donkey traveling to town to sell vegetables from her garden

CHAPTER 11

Haiti: Land of Conflict and Tears

Those who sow in tears will reap with songs of joy. Those who go out weeping carrying seed to sow, will return with songs of joy, carrying sheaves with them. Psalms 126: 5, 6 (NIV)

As I said before, when God called me to go to Haiti, I knew absolutely nothing about the country. I didn't know that Haiti was located approximately 700 miles south of Miami, Florida, and just east of Cuba in the Caribbean Sea. Now after visiting Haiti for the past 42 years and living there for 36 of those years, I have learned a lot about one of the poorest nations on earth. Perhaps a little background on this country would be helpful in understanding both the culture we live in and some of the struggles we encounter.

Haiti, like America, was first discovered by Christopher Columbus on his first visit to the New World in December 1492. Slightly smaller than the state of Maryland, Haiti was part of the island named by Columbus as "La Isla Espanola" (The Spanish Island), which was later changed to Hispaniola. Columbus established a makeshift settlement on the northern coast of the island which he dubbed Navidad (Christmas) when his flagship Santa Maria struck a coral reef and foundered near the site of present-day Cap-Haïtien. At that time, the island was inhabited by the Taino Indians (or Arawak) who referred to their home as "Hayti"or "Ayti," both translated as "mountainous" land.[4]

The next few centuries of Hispaniola's colorful history are both sad and plagued by political violence from Spain, France, and Great Britain, all wanting the fertile land that produced cocoa, cotton, sugar cane, and coffee, and the gold they thought lay beneath the surface.

The Spaniards, through Columbus' discovery, recognized the value of the gold trinkets the Indians were wearing and had expectations of readily accessible gold reserves on the island. When this proved unfounded, Hispaniola, called Santo Domingo under the Spanish dominion, still was important as a seat of colonizing other territories and became the first outpost of the Spanish Empire. Thus, it became a laboratory to develop policies for governing new possessions. But its prominence in the world soon lost its power as forced labor, abuse, disease against which the Indians had no immunity, and the growth of the mixed European and Indian population contributed to the elimination of the Taino and their culture. With no natives to work the land, the landowners moved on to other territories.

A new era began in the 16th century when French settlers brought African slaves to the island to work the sugar fields. By this time, the native Indians had practically disappeared, and slave labor seemed to be an answer to a landowner's prayer.

With the slaves from the west coast of South Africa, came the religious practices of voodoo, which were more of a lifestyle tradition than a religion. The French treated the African slaves with undue harshness, creating hatred amid an already resentful environment. From the sexual relations of the white slave owners and the slaves came a class of light-skinned Negroes called Mulattoes. All of these factors would later result in a large number of problems for the small island of Hispaniola.

Hispaniola, in the 18th century, was regarded as the most valuable tropical colony of its size in the world and was the largest sugar producer in the West Indies. It was also strategically important as the gateway to the Caribbean region. However, the wealth of Hispaniola was based on slavery, and the planters were aware of the dangers of rebellion. After the French Revolution (1789-1799), when slavery was radically redefined in France, the French Landowners in Hispaniola defensively called for more freedom to run their colony as they wished. The white French landowners refused to implement the new slave decrees by the French Government that gave their slaves more freedom, and soon Whites, Mulattoes, and Negroes all were fighting with shifting alliances and mutual hatred for each other.

Out of the chaos rose a new leader, an ex-slave called Francois-Dominique Toussaint, who created his own roaming army. After several revolts, Toussaint became the first person of African descent to head a Republic. However, Toussaint's reign was short lived as was the other revolts and takeovers that occurred for the remainder of the 19th century. It was also during the 19th century that the Island of Hispaniola split into two countries: Haiti on the west side of the island and Dominican Republic on the east side.

At the beginning of the 20th century, the United States became financially and politically involved in the small country of Haiti, for geopolitical and strategic reasons. Intervention in 1915 was provoked by the murder and mutilation of a president, but U.S. occupation brought order and the reorganization of public finances. Although this occupation provided for health services, paved roads, water and sewage systems, and education for its children, the occupation was not received kindly by the Haitians. Once again the Haitians found themselves in an occupied state, and the rulers were white. This resulted in even greater power for the lighter skinned Mulattos. Haitians, as a whole, resented the U.S. occupation, and from 1918 to 1920, several uprisings resulted in the loss of over 2,000 Haitians lives.

When the American occupation ceased in 1934, the country was still in shambles. There was the ever-constant struggle for power between the Catholic Church and the followers of voodoo. By this time, the abuse of the land in previous centuries had left it barren of vegetation and trees. Now, Haiti was overpopulated with very few natural resources to sustain its inhabitants.

In 1957, Francois (Papa Doc) Duvalier, a black nationalist, was elected president, and in the subsequent 1964 election, he declared that he was elected for life. Duvalier, unlike some of his predecessors, managed to hold on to his power. Duvalier's power rested on the use of an armed militia, the Tontons Macoutes, to dominate the people. Tens of thousands of Haitians were murdered, and thousands more fled the country. Papa Doc died in 1971, and Jean-Claude Duvalier (Baby Doc) inherited his father's position. Repression eased somewhat, though dissidence rose encouraged partly by U.S. policies on human rights. The battle for power continued between Whites and Negroes, Whites and Mulattos, and Negroes and Mulattos.

It was under Baby Doc's regime and this political climate that we entered Haiti in 1976.

Chapter 12

Adjusting to Culture Shock

Now he who supplies seed to the sower and bread for food will also supply and increase your store of seed and will enlarge the harvest of your righteousness. 2 Corinthians 9:10 (NIV)

ON 1976, THERE were two distinct classes in Haiti: rich and poor, or the *have* and the *have-nots*. We were definitely in the latter class where material possessions were concerned. But to the Haitians, all thought we were rich just because we were Americans. Hence, we were always being asked to give help. We were rich abundantly in the spiritual blessings from God, but financially, we were completely dependent upon God's moving on the hearts of individuals or churches to help support our ministry.

Reflecting back on that period of our life, I really don't know how we managed to make ends meet on the small amount of money we received from donations. But we did. And, I know beyond a shadow of doubt that God always was the source who supplied our needs. After we received the check for $800, other checks of support began to arrive daily, and we were able to pay our bills and begin our ministry. One day we received a check for $1,000, and we thought we had "died and gone to heaven!"

One thing we discovered quickly about the Haitian people's mindset is that they believe in survival and doing so in any way possible. Asking for help from "rich" Americans is not considered beneath their dignity. Sometimes this survival instinct even includes pretending to get converted to Christianity in order to get a job or a handout. They do what they feel they have to do in order to survive. It is a pretty daunting task to determine who the true believers are from those who are only seeking other types of help. To succeed in this endeavor and not be fooled, we recognized the necessity for relying on the wisdom God gave us; we had to be able to accurately discern each person's intent.

Because of the language barrier, the first few years of trying to tell the real Christians from the pretend ones were very difficult for us. Our family took Creole lessons from teachers at the American Haitian Institute because this was the only place where Americans were taught how to speak Creole. Every day we attended classes where Creole was the only language spoken the entire time. Often I would get so tired of hearing Creole that I just wanted everyone to shut up! It is annoying to hear a language constantly being spoken when you don't know what is being said.

There were special words we learned to use when we were preaching, and there were special words we learned that pertained to the construction business that were not used any place else. In addition, there were medical terms we had to learn in order to help the people. We had to learn the *whole* language. As a result, we continued to practice speaking the Haitian language to everyone all the time. It took about two years before we could speak the Creole comfortably to everyone all the time. But by then, it had become *our* language too. Even now, having spoken Creole for more than 35 years and thinking I can hold my own in conversations, occasionally someone will say something that I just don't understand. When that happens, I just nod my head and smile, hoping a reply isn't expected.

Once we started using the language in everyday life, our job got easier. Joyce and I continued with the lessons, but the girls picked up the language a lot quicker just by talking with their friends. Cindy had taken a few French lessons in high school, which helped her communicate better in Creole than any of us. Both girls were enrolled at Quisqueya Christian School where everyone spoke English. There were lots of children whose parents were missionaries who attended this school, but there were also children whose parents were ambassadors and business workers. For many different reasons, all these people wanted their children to go to school with English-speaking teachers.

There were many major culture adjustments, the most important one being getting accustomed to the food. Not only is the food different, it is generally unsanitary. The major amount of food is bought in open-air markets where flies, mosquitoes, and gnats eat their share first before the food is sold. When we ate at friends' homes, we were sick frequently. Clean water is something we had taken for granted in the States, but in Haiti, it was a luxury. It didn't take Joyce long to learn the best places to shop. She learned quickly how to "boil" water (excuse the pun) and take other needed precautions with the food she prepared.

The transportation system in Haiti is quite different from any other kind in the world. Forget an air-conditioned bus or train. If you do not have your own vehicle, the only way to get from one place to another is to walk or ride a Tap-Tap. Tap-Taps are small and, mostly, old, old, old pickup trucks with the truck bed pretty much gutted. Passengers sit on benches built on both sides of the bed and sometimes in the middle. Railings stretch across the top and sides of the truck bed for holding on to by standing passengers who don't want to be bumped out of the Tap-Tap. Colorful pictures are painted all over the back, front, and sides of the truck. Every square inch contains some form of writing or advertisement. Some trucks even have Scripture verses written on them. Needless to say, none are enclosed or air-conditioned. Anyone and anything are allowed to ride, as long as the fare is paid when you hop on. It is common for farmers coming in from the surrounding towns to ride in with their pigs, goats, and chickens. The aroma in the back of the Tap-Tap can become quite rich very quickly when you are sharing a ride with a farmer and his animals on his way to the market.

There are set schedules for these Tap-Taps; you just have to learn what they are. Tap-Taps are everywhere, so you just look for one that is going where you want to go, flag it down, and jump in. Quickly! With only one vehicle for our family, Joyce and the girls had to ride the Tap-Taps pretty often. In order to get to and from school, sometimes the girls had to make connections on several Tap-Taps. When we first arrived in Haiti, riding a Tap-Tap might have been uncomfortable and smelly, but we never feared for our safety. However, in recent years, we stick to riding only in our own vehicles. Unfortunately, the safety climate has been altered by the high rate of crime.

These were just a few of the adjustments we had to make living in our new country. We felt it was a small price to pay for seeing souls won to the Lord.

A typical Tap Tap, public transportation, on the streets of Port-au-Prince

CHAPTER 13

Where Should We Start and What Do We Need to Do?

Ask the Lord of the harvest, therefore, to send out workers into his harvest field. Matthew 9:38 (NIV)

𝒰NLIKE MOST MISSIONARIES who go out to a mission field, we did not have any support or instruction from a specific denomination or organization showing us how to start our ministry. We had no "missionary handbook" in English or Creole with step-by-step instructions to follow. It certainly would have been easier if we had received at least some guidelines to go by when we first arrived in Haiti, but we didn't. And I would never encourage anyone today to go to a mission field in the same way we did. Our walk into the mission field was done purely by faith in a mighty God! I am so glad He did not show us everything He wanted and expected us to do in the beginning, because I might not have been up to handling it all. If He had, most likely, I would have choked, thrown up my hands, and quit! *God has been faithful to just show us what we needed to know at the time we needed to know it.*

At the beginning our ministry in Haiti, not being affiliated with any particular denomination or organization did make things more difficult for us. However, once word got around that Joyce and I were missionaries, people came from all over Haiti inviting us to come out to their brush arbor church and see if we would help them establish a more permanent church or school building.

Before I go any further, I would like to explain the term "brush arbor." It is simply an established gathering place where families and friends in a particular area meet together to worship God. Generally, the brush arbor is in some far away station or remote area from town where the inhabitants are so poor they cannot support a pastor. The word "brush" comes from any type of tree or bush that is readily available. This "brush" is then used to cover poles or sticks to provide some type of protection from the sun. The word "arbor" refers to any type of overhead shelter. Some groups may hold worship services in an actual brush arbor structure made of palm leaves that have been stretched over poles. Sometimes services are conducted outside in uncovered open areas. There may be some crudely built benches made out of coconut trees or some cane chairs for people to sit on, but some groups just sit on the ground.

Some brush arbor church congregations have been around for years, praying and hoping someday that some missionary will build them a permanent church building and provide a full-time pastor. Usually, the weekly speaker at a brush arbor church is a local church member who has the most knowledge of the Word of God and is willing to share his experience with the others. Or, the speaker may be the only one in the village who has a Bible and can read.

Every ministry has a starting place, and ours was reaching out to the lady who sold us vegetables in the market place, as well as giving to any neighbor who needed help. We tried not to miss an opportunity to share with anyone the reason why we had come to

Haiti. We ministered to people with whom we had daily contact. Then, when someone told us of a specific need, we would go out into the villages to give whatever help we could. We relied upon God to place on our hearts the specific needs of the Haitian people.

One of the first villages we visited was called Boutin. Boutin is located in the central part of the island and is about 40 miles from Port-au-Prince. The population of Boutin and its surrounding areas varies, but when we began ministering there, approximately 20,000 people called the "cul-de-sac" home. A prolonged drought in this area at the time we had first visited had brought about massive devastation and starvation. The road to Boutin was nothing more than an established path in the dirt. Some of the surrounding areas had no paths at all.

We began our ministry in Boutin by bringing in a few food items such as beans and rice. I borrowed a horse and saddle to carry these supplies to the people suffering from the drought. In this farming community, the people who had depended upon the gardens to sustain their existence were now starving. During those visits, I took time to tell the people where the food came from and how much God loved them.

Daughter Faithe and John during a visit to Boutin

One man who lived in Boutin was called Papa Joey Constant. Papa Joey was about 70 years old and a Christian. We became friends quickly and he agreed to let me use his porch to preach about Jesus to the people in the village of Boutin. I remember that period of time well as I stood on Papa Joey's porch in front of an old table I used as a podium, and spoke through a translator to a small congregation. Later on, we built a covering in his yard with a few poles covered by palm leaves to keep out the scorching sun. The memories of our early-day experiences with all the hardships and difficulties are like treasures that have been stored away. Sometimes I replay those scenes in my mind and am completely awed by the sheer magnitude of how far my faithful God has brought us!

When you are helping people—no matter how small that help might be—it does not take long for those people to begin feeling comfortable around you. Soon, the people began bringing their sick children or relatives to us for prayer. And we did lay hands on them and prayed for God to touch them. But while we were praying, we couldn't help but notice a cut or laceration on an arm that needed only a few stitches to make it better, or a rash that needed only some antibiotic ointment to clear it up. We could not help but feel that with the right medical supplies, WE could be the answer to the prayers we were praying.

While I was working for the FMC Ordinance Plant in West Virginia, in the mid to late 1960s, I had received a small amount of medical training. Joyce, having always been interested in medicine, knew a little about what to do in certain medical situations as well. We tried to attend to any of the medical needs we were qualified to handle with the small amount of medical supplies we always carried along with us. No, we didn't have any medical degrees, but you have to understand that *any* kind of medical assistance is better than *none* in Haiti. Before attending to an injury, Joyce nor I have ever had anyone ask to see our medical diplomas.

Our medical clinic at Boutin was started with $20. It was a gift Joyce's mom had sent her with instructions to buy anything she wanted. When the money arrived, there were so many things the family could use that it was hard for Joyce to decide what to buy. Instead, she went to the pharmacy and bought as many antibiotics and medical supplies she could with the $20, and we took them with us on our next trip to Boutin.

At Boutin, Papa Joey gave us a room in a little grass hut with a dirt floor, and that day we started seeing our first patients on a regular basis. Many babies have been born in that little grass hut, and many children with high fevers have been doctored and helped in that crude surrounding.

One day, a pregnant lady came to our little grass hut for medical assistance. Her delivery was a little more complicated than we felt we could handle. The umbilical cord was wrapped around the baby's neck, and we feared if we didn't get professional help, the mother and baby might die. We packed everyone in our truck and headed for the hospital at Port-au-Prince.

During this particular trip to Boutin, we had a visiting nurse from Missouri who was with us, and she accompanied us in the truck. The nurse kept asking us to stop on the way to the hospital to see how the baby was doing. I knew it didn't matter how that baby was doing, because we couldn't help it. We didn't have the medical knowledge needed, so we were doing the best thing possible for the mother and baby and that was getting to the hospital as fast as we could over those bumpy and washed out roads. All we could do was pray for God to get us to the hospital in time where trained medical help could take over.

Once we arrived at the hospital and secured medical help for our patient, we left and went home. Later on that evening, we received word that mother and baby were doing fine. Just having a small part in helping a mother and child survive made all our efforts worthwhile.

There were so many medical needs we knew we were not qualified to handle, so we began inviting doctors from the States to come and visit us. One of the first doctors to come and work in our medical clinic was Dr. Howard Thomas and his dear wife, Ann, from Savannah, Tennessee. During each visit, they spent many long hours taking care of patients. When they took a break, they would teach Joyce how to stitch up wounds for people who had been cut or punctured. Each time doctors visited our clinic, Joyce would glean as much medical information from them as her mind could hold.

Every year more and more doctors came to work in our clinic, and they brought other doctors with them. Once a doctor visits and sees the needs here, he or she is never the same. Sometimes we are fortunate enough to have not only a medical doctor arrive but an optometrist or a dentist. The clinic hours are long and hard, but we try never to turn anyone away who needs medical treatment. In the past 36 years, we have had many medical teams come and help with the clinics. Our medical ministry has been a tremendous witness to the people of Haiti of the love God has for them.

I remember an incident that happened in our early years in Haiti. One evening when my father was visiting us from the States, we heard a pounding on our front door. We opened it to see a man standing there who had been cut deeply on his leg near his ankle by a machete knife. We didn't take time to get the story of how he was cut but quickly cleared off the dining room table, covered it with a piece of plastic, and laid the man on the table. I disinfected the wound and stitched it up, and the man went on his way. We learned later that his wound had healed nicely. My actions blew my Dad's mind!

CHAPTER 14

Building the First
School and Church

*Where there are no oxen, the manager is empty, but from the
strength of an ox come abundant harvests. Proverbs 14:4 (NIV)*

D URING OUR WEEKLY trips to Boutin, we discovered there
wasn't anyone in the village that could read or write! We
knew education of any kind was a serious need at Boutin, and our
hearts were heavy with the desire to do something about it. However,
we had no funds to build a school. But, by faith, we started a school
anyway. We held our first school under the palm trees in Papa Joey's
front yard, the same place where the people came to listen to me
preach. We found a couple of teachers who were qualified to teach
and paid them a small salary to teach the 19 students who had come
to our school to learn. We held school every day under this brush
arbor dwelling of poles and coconut limbs.

Pastor Earl Cox, our former pastor in Alexandria, Virginia, who had been very much against our moving to Haiti, had stayed in touch with us. When he realized we were serious about our calling and that God was blessing our efforts, we shared with him the needs of the people of Boutin. Every Sunday morning, Pastor Cox had a radio program that aired in Alexandria. He began sharing our stories with his radio audience. Touched by our primitive school stories, his radio audience began sending him money to help us build a permanent school building in Boutin. With Pastor Cox's help and the donations from his radio audience, we built a ten-room building that held over 700 children. In two of those rooms, we housed our medical clinic.

After the school building was built, we knew we had to build a permanent church. Our brush arbor congregation had grown considerably in the past couple of years, and we realized it was now time for a permanent building. We began construction of our first church at Boutin. This church was built with funds sent to us from churches and individuals who had heard us speak during the summer months when we returned home. After being in Haiti a few months, we quickly realized we would need to have some regular, dependable financial support in order to continue our ministry there. The best way to get this support was to return to the States and tell churches and individuals of the great needs of the Haitian people and the work that God had helped us accomplish. So, each year, we left Haiti and returned home to spend two or three months during the summer raising funds for our personal support and the support of the churches and schools. Today, we still continue these summer visits.

During the "missionary services," as the churches would call our visits, Joyce and the girls would sing in Creole and share our stories of what God was doing for the people of Haiti. Many congregations were touched and moved by our ministry and pledged support. Some individuals even felt led to send us a monthly donation. This is how it has worked for over 36 years. We lived then and now on just the support we get in the mail.

As soon as we had received enough funds, we would build another church. I have started the foundation of some of our churches with only faith in our pockets. And we all know that faith isn't really faith until it is all you are hanging onto! With true faith on our side, God always supplied the exact amount of money we needed to complete the building. We have never had to stop construction because of lack of funds. But please keep in mind that we never went into a building project unless we were a 100 percent sure we had received the OK from God to start on the project. Getting that OK from God took a lot of fasting and prayer for us to feel confident about what God was saying. A person can have good intentions and want to do good things, but that person needs to make sure those good intentions line up with God's plans.

With so many needs in Haiti, it has always been difficult determining which outstation or brush arbor church would be next on our list for erecting a permanent building. After much prayer and fasting, some decisions to build came easier than others, like the one at Cotin.

We were in the process of building our first permanent church at Boutin when the pastor from the neighboring village of Cotin came over and introduced himself as Pastor Charles. Cotin is a town about 20 miles south of Boutin where many people at that time had never ever seen white people. Many of the inhabitants there had been taught that white people were more of a spirit or ghost than a real person.

Pastor Charles came over every week during our clinic day at Boutin and watched the progress on the Boutin church. During every visit, he would take me aside and beg for help at his church; they needed a permanent building, too. He pleaded for me to come and speak to his congregation on Sunday. I would reply that I didn't have the money to help him, but I would pray for God to send someone to him.

After much pleading from Pastor Charles, Joyce and I visited the Cotin brush arbor church, and like our first church at Boutin, it was nothing more than a few poles with palm leaves wrapped around them. With us that day in Cotin was a visiting group from a small country church in Buchannon, West Virginia, whose pastor was Rev. Carolyn Groves. The congregation at Cotin consisted of about 125 people, and with this large congregation, I could see the definite need for a permanent church. I can still visualize the whites of those people's eyes who stood on the outside of the crudely built brush arbor church, peering at us through those palm leaves—questioning, hoping, begging for us to do something. I could sense the hunger these people had for God and felt their desire to obtain more knowledge. Pastor Groves was so moved by the hunger these people had for the Word of God, she went home and told her church about the need of the Cotin Christians. Pastor Groves' congregation sent enough money to build Pastor Charles a permanent church in Cotin!

Ethel Painter, who was 90 years old and from Stanley, Virginia, had been another visitor to Cotin that day. After her trip to Haiti and, especially her visit to Cotin, Ethel became a big supporter of our ministry.

When we first started going to Cotin to build their church, the people in the village were terrified of Joyce, our girls, and me. As I mentioned before, many of them thought we were ghosts or spirits. When we drove into the town, if the mothers saw us they would grab their children and take them into their huts and shut their doors. To keep us out, they put baskets of voodoo items (such as chicken feathers or cloth with rice) in front of their door. Since Haitians are afraid to cross over any voodoo basket, they probably thought we would be afraid to cross over too. Sometimes the people hung voodoo baskets in a bush or tree. I would take those baskets and run over them with my truck or smash them with my feet to show the people I was not afraid of their voodoo spirits. I tried to teach them that the power of Christ is stronger than voodoo. Voodoo is a tradition that has been passed down from one generation to another. It takes a very long time to get a Haitian to fully believe that Christ is stronger than voodoo. Through the miracles of Christ working in our ministry, many Haitians have turned from their voodoo practices to believing completely and solely in the power of Christ.

As time went on, God just kept sending people our way to supply the money needed to build permanent structures for our brush arbor churches.

In Haiti, as in many other places, the needs outnumbered the funds available. Sometimes at night, after we had done all we could do during the day, we wept over the souls and the poverty that was ever before us. Often, we had to cut back on our feeding programs in the school, because we did not have the money. There were times when we watched children die because they didn't have enough to eat. Even though we knew it was not possible to help everyone, we still desired to help all we could. God continued to bless the work of our hands. In order not to become discouraged that we couldn't help everyone, we had to be thankful for the miracles and blessings that were happening as a result of souls being saved.

One particular blessing happened in the Guibert church where I was preaching in a revival. The Guibert church sits down in a valley, and because no road had been built going down to the church, we had to park about a fourth of a mile from the church. Every night as we walked that quarter mile down the hill to the church, a voodoo priest, who was paralyzed from his waist down because of some poison he had taken during a voodoo service, sat by the roadside about 300 yards from the service. We had set up a speaker system for the services, hoping that everyone around could hear our preaching. After the service each night, as we left for home, the voodoo priest would call out obscenities to us and ridicule us for our belief in Christ.

One night after the revival service ended, as we walked back up the hill to our vehicle, it was so dark you could not see your hands in front of you. I was mulling over in my mind the sermon I had just preached on Naaman and his healing from God, when this voodoo priest called out to me.

"Hey Pastor," he says to me, "I heard you preaching tonight about God healing that man. If God will heal me, I will serve him."

There didn't seem to be any heckling in his tone of voice now, but my first fast thought was "Hey, buddy, you don't bargain with God." But I held my tongue and went over to where he was sitting. I prayed a simple prayer for God to heal him. Nothing happened, and we left and walked on up the hill to our vehicle.

The next morning about 6:00 a.m., the pastor of the Guibert church came to my home to tell me the good news. Through all his excitement, he managed to tell me how the voodoo priest came walking down the dusty road to his house at 4:30 that morning, healed by the power of almighty God. Praise God! This type of miracle is what brings true revival. Jesus Christ is the same yesterday, today, and forever! Amen! The voodoo priest had accepted Christ as his Savior. And once he had asked Christ into his heart and life, he brought all his vast supply of voodoo paraphernalia he used in his voodoo services to the pastor at Guibert and told him, "I don't need this anymore!"

This is just one of the many stories of lives we have seen that have been changed by the power of Jesus Christ. As we would get the reports from our churches each month, we rejoiced in the large number of souls being saved. This was why we were here. We wanted—no, we needed—for God to save souls from eternal damnation and set them free from their load of sin and guilt. Seeing people healed was just an added bonus and a witness to the goodness of the God we served. Bringing the Good News of Christ's salvation was the true mission God had called us to do.

During our annual summer visits to the States, we began inviting the pastors of the churches where we preached to come to Haiti and bring a group with them so they could see first-hand what we were doing in Haiti. From my own personal experience, I knew how important it was to know where your money goes when you make a donation. Over the years, we found there were a lot of wonderful Christians in the United States who desired to give to God's work, but they wanted to know where their money was going, and they wanted to know it was being used where someone said it was being used. I can not tell you how often, during one of our church visits, someone would come up to me and say, "Brother John, there are so many ministers and pastors out there asking for money to help people in other lands that we just don't know who we can trust."

I knew if we could get people to come Haiti and they could see what we were doing with their money, they would go back and testify to others, and more support would come in for our ministry. And this philosophy has been proven true. Once a pastor or group came to Haiti and saw how our ministry was growing and how much good we were doing in spreading the Gospel of Jesus Christ, it was easy for them to go back and ask their congregations or friends to help us out. Sometimes the visit by a church group was just that: a sightseeing visit. Sometimes the group that visited would work on a school or church project such as building benches or constructing desks. But the most important aspect of people visiting us was for them to bear witness to the work that was being done with the money that had been sent to us. We encouraged pastors to bring members of their congregations as well as other pastors. And today, we still employ this same method to raise funds to support our ministry. Now, during our annual June to September trip to the States, we visit anywhere between 50 and 60 churches whose pastors and congregations have been to Haiti to see our ministry.

Warning! Once you have been here, you are hooked for life.

Dedication of Terre Rouge Church donated by Precision Pump Co. of Cross Lanes, WV. Pictured left to right: Haitian Pastors Faniel Altidor and Pastor Jean Dinel Elie, Darrell Huffman, Haitian Pastor Joseph Constant, Joyce Hanson, Pastor John Hanson, Jeremy Kemerer, (hidden) Kevin Kemerer, Deona Kemerer, Barry Kemerer, Eurlene Kemerer and Paul Bailey.

CHAPTER 15

Building a Bible School

Remember this: whoever sows sparingly will also reap sparingly, and whoever sows generously will also reap generously. 2 Corinthians 9:6 (NIV)

WHEN WE FIRST arrived in Haiti, we met and had fellowship with missionaries who were affiliated with specific denominations or organizations. It was typical for missionaries to get together as a support group and discuss what progress was being made and any problems or situations that were being encountered. In the beginning, we were invited to these groups, and the people made an effort to get to know us by asking many questions. One of the first questions asked was, "Where did you go to school?" And the second was, "Who are you affiliated with?"

When Joyce and I explained that we hadn't gone to school anywhere, and we weren't affiliated with any group or denomination but had been called by God to come to Haiti, the surprise always showed in their faces. I knew they were thinking, "Boy, you won't last long around here!" And to be completely truthful, we soon realized these missionaries really did not want to have much to do with us. We did not have the right credentials. Because of this, in this strange country and among strange people, sometimes we felt like outcasts among our own peers.

We were hurt by this attitude, but we had been given a mission, and that is what we concentrated on. Several years later, some of these same organizations that had not accepted us in the beginning began coming to us for help and assistance. We opened our hearts and home to these dear people. God has His timing for everything. You just have to keep your eyes and hearts on what He has called you to do and not be influenced by what other people do and say.

Experience is the best teacher; from our experience of how we were treated, we have done our best to make sure any new missionaries we meet are treated with lots of love and understanding. We realize how important it is to help them feel they are a special part of God's work in Haiti.

In the fellowship groups, there was one guy by the name of Ron Bolen from Dayton, Ohio, whom I had gotten to know. Ron worked for an organization called International Missions (IM). IM had been operating in Haiti since 1974, but it was in the process of shutting down its work in Haiti. Ron confided to me that IM was leaving because they were discouraged and that he just did not have a heart or a burden for the work in Haiti any more.

Discouragement is a common emotion with missionaries anywhere. You have to understand that conditions here are usually terrible at best. It is hard to operate when funds are scarce and you do not have the right tools to do the job. Unless you are 100 percent positive you have received the missionary calling on your life, doubt and discouragement can set in and destroy you. And, even if you are sure of your calling, when making progress on the mission field runs slowly, discouragement can destroy your ministry.

Ron asked if I and another individual would be interested in taking over IM and continuing it as an organization along with taking the churches and outstations they had already established. IM was already registered with the government and was recognized as a legitimate non-profit organization. This was a good thing for us since it generally took a lot of paper work, money, and time to get recognized by the Haitian government.

In 1977, we agreed to take over the IM organization and the management of those churches as well as any programs in which the churches were involved. There were three other ministries that were part of IM, and all of these ministries agreed to our plan to continue to support IM. Pastor Sammy Huff, from Detroit, Michigan, was the leader of one of those ministries, and today, he continues to serve on our board.

IM had started brush arbor churches in Robin, Lefèrve, and Blanchard, all about an hour's drive from Port-au-Prince. There was another brush arbor church in Robin where Pastor Sammy Huff and his mother, Hulda Huff, had interests in helping and working. "Mama" Huff, as everyone calls her, is still active in assisting and gathering items to send to Haiti along with her financial assistance. There was also a permanent church building in Guibert.

After we assumed the responsibilities for IM, there were some negative things that happened in IM's leadership that we knew must change. So, Joyce and I began clearing up the things that needed to be corrected. In 1977, we changed the name to International Missions Outreach so we could have a fresh start in rebuilding the integrity and respectability of this ministry. From that time forward, we have been International Missions Outreach (IMO), and we have guarded our integrity diligently.

When churches in the States started supporting our ministry in Haiti, we were able to begin building more churches. We didn't push for people to support *us* as much as we encouraged people to build and support the churches. One of those generous supporters was

Ed Unicume, a businessman from Spokane, Washington. Ed built condos, sold real estate, and had rental property as well. The first time he came to visit us in Haiti, we stayed up talking to 1:00 a.m. at the Le Regent Hotel in Port-au-Prince. Early on in our ministry, this was where everyone stayed when they came to visit us in Haiti. We did not have any facilities at that time to house our visitors, and everyone had to pay their own hotel bill.

In the first five years of our ministry, we built seven permanent churches—five of them at the places where brush arbor churches had been started by IM, and two churches at Boutin and Cotin, where we had established our own brush arbor churches. In addition, we built the elementary school at Boutin. During Ed's and his wife, Donna's, first visit, they became very interested in what we were doing. They really understood all the building and construction jargon and what it took physically and financially to create buildings. But even better, they understood spiritually how important it was to build in the Kingdom of God. God always sends the right people at the right time. Ed and Donna were our "right" people.

After their first visit, Ed and Donna were loyal supporters. Often they would call me and discuss what project we were thinking about. Shortly after our conversation, they would send me a check to help cover our expenses. Ed and Donna were a very wealthy couple, but should you pass them on the street, you would think they were just as ordinary as you and me. The Lord so graciously brought them into our lives through another loyal supporter named Dave Gourley, who had worked with Ed in another ministry in the states. Dave and Ed sang together in a group with this ministry. Over the years, the links on the chain that connected all of us to IMO kept multiplying. God kept bringing more pastors, laypeople, and businessmen our way to help with the work He had called us to do.

At the end of 1980, on another visit to Haiti, Ed and I were seated at a restaurant talking about our building programs. The more I talked, the more Ed sensed something different was going on in my mind. I am always thinking four to five years down the road about where we feel God may be leading us, because I believe that "where there is no vision, the people perish" (Proverbs 29:18, KJV). I confessed to Ed that I believed God wanted us to build a Bible school to train our pastors and church workers. I told him that we have these churches now, but we don't have trained pastors and teachers who can preach and teach the Word of God. I went on to explain that, for the most part, Sunday School consisted of someone reading a Scripture verse, and the class would repeat it over and over again until everyone memorized it. That was Sunday School. When the main service started, each class would get up and recite that memory verse together.

Most of our churches did not have qualified pastors. The process we had for acquiring pastors was for us to spend time working in the community, and the Christian individual who showed the most potential as a leader was chosen as pastor of the church. It was not a very sound way to choose a pastor, but it was the only way we knew that would work.

"We need a Bible school to train and teach our people how to be pastors and teachers!" I emphasized to Ed.

Ed listened patiently to what my heart was saying, and when I stopped for a breath of air, all he said was, "What do you have in mind?"

I quickly reached for a napkin off the table and drew up the Bible school plans I had in my head. I didn't even have any property in mind at this time, but I drew a rough building plan of what God had laid on my heart. My drawing was simple; it consisted of a few squares that represented the buildings we would need to house, feed, and educate our future pastors and teachers. Excitement ran through me like a bolt of lightning. The vision God gave me for a Bible school was about to come alive! Faithe Ann, our youngest daughter, who is now our Operation and Office Manager in the USA office in Clendenin, West Virginia, once gave me a little plaque that said, "Only those who see the invisible can do the impossible." I have kept those words in my heart ever since!

Ed went home and had an architect draw up some real plans. Then we printed up some cards announcing our new Bible school. It took a while to find just the right property, but I found an acre of land located in Delmas outside of Port-au-Prince for $37,000. Wow! Land was costly here, but as the old saying goes, they just are not making any more of it—especially on an island in the middle of the Caribbean!

Between Ed's and my dad's donations, we bought the land which was to become the first part of our headquarters in Delmas. In July 1982, at our Third Annual International Missions Outreach Convention held at the Reality Gospel Church in Alexandria, Virginia, almost $18,000 was pledged to help build our Bible school. Dr. Jerry Goff raised that amount from the congregation in the Wednesday night service. We were on our way! That was in our early beginnings. It does not seem like a great deal of money today, but at that time when we were just starting out, we thought we had hit pay dirt. Remember, if God cannot trust you in the small things, you will never get a chance to go on to the bigger things.

The first thing built on the acre at Delmas was a wall around the property. Walls are built to keep your building supplies safe. This is a cultural thing. If you don't have a wall around your property, people feel they can come and "borrow" anything you have. But when you put up a wall, even if they still have access to the property, they will not bother your things. In Haiti, for the most part, people respect the wall and what it stands for.

So, our wall went up to protect our building supplies, however, all the funds needed for the actual building had not yet been received. It had always been my policy not to start a project until all the funds had been secured. But, on this project, I believed God wanted me to go ahead and begin building and to have faith that the remainder of the funds would come in.

Every time a pastor brought in a group for a visit, I would take them out to my little ex-cornfield/trash dump acre and expound on the Bible school we were going to build. There was no road leading up to the property, so we had to traipse through the field, stepping on whatever trash had been left behind by previous owners. I would stand in the middle of the field and point out where all the various buildings would be situated, including the building that would house the students. Some of the visitors would say, "Praise the Lord, that's great," but I could tell they were not seeing my vision, and that was okay. I had seen the vision, and I knew it would come to pass, because God had given it to me.

As we began to receive the funds, we started building our Bible school. Once construction was started, our visitors began to get a glimpse of the vision, and they wanted to jump in and help. Always remember when times are tough, if you just keep going and moving in the direction God is showing you, He will supply the people that are needed.

In December 1984, we completed construction of our new Bible school and then held the dedication service. Pastor Richard Edgar, from Charleston, South Carolina, and Pastor H. K. McKnight, from Savannah, Georgia, were our guest speakers. There were several missionary visitors that day, but we were especially privileged to have Ed and Donna Unicume with us, for they had shared the Bible school vision with me. It was a glorious day of celebration and thanksgiving for what God had done and was continuing to do in our ministry in Haiti.

Going to Bible school is not an easy decision for anyone to make. It takes a firm determination from the students to succeed. If students are not truly serious about serving the Lord in a ministerial or pastoral role, they usually quit before the first year is completed. To graduate from our Bible school is a large and difficult task, and only those truly called by God to be ministers or teachers are able to accomplish it.

The way the Bible school system works is unique. Each student goes to school for one week and then returns home to work for one week. A semester lasts 12 weeks, with three semesters in each school year. To earn a diploma, a student must complete three years of class work. At any given time, there are three classes operating: a first-year class; a second-year class; and a third-year class. Using this schedule, we have pastors and teachers graduating every year.

At the beginning of their education, we explain clearly to the students that we cannot promise them financial support while they attend Bible school nor can we promise them a job after graduation. However, through the general fund, IMO does all it can to give these students as much support as possible, because the mission to evangelize the people of Haiti is the most important mission of all.

This on-again/off-again system enables the men to continue working to support their families. This length of time also gives me a good opportunity to get to know the students and determine how each one can best be used in God's work. By the end of the three years, I am able to assess who is serious about being a pastor or teacher and who is using this avenue as a way out of poverty. We also inform all Bible school students who come from other organizations that when they have completed their time here and earned their diploma, they must return to their own organization; IMO will not accept them. We teach our students that possessing integrity, good character, and respectability speaks much louder than any message they will ever preach.

Every year there is a special week set aside for our Haitian church pastors where guest pastors from the States are brought to the Bible school to speak on specific topics of interest. This is a separate event from our Bible school program, but it is held at our Bible school facilities. This special week of teaching is always a great blessing to our pastors. They not only receive good teaching on different topics and ways of doing things in ministry, but they get to come together corporately and fellowship with one another. They share with each other what is going on in their own churches, and they pray with all the other pastors. So often pastors in the remote areas feel they are out there alone because of the distance that separates them from us, as well as the lack of transportation to and from their areas. At IMO, we try very hard to let them know how much we appreciate and care for them and believe in the ministries they have in their areas.

On any given Bible school class day, the atmosphere is charged with anticipation—anticipation in what God is going to do next! I love to watch the students as they find their way to their classes, knowing each class will bring them closer to the God who loved them enough to provide this school for them. I love it when students come up to me and tell me how "life changing" this experience has been and how much closer they have become to God. I love it when I pass out the diplomas and feel the excitement in the air, knowing this is a new and precious beginning for many of these students. They have been given a chance to change not only their lives, but to help change the lives of others. I love my God who is so good!

We began Bible classes in October 1985, and to date, we have graduated over 8,000 students. Hundreds of these students have come from other denominations. We trained them and returned them to their homes full of the Word and Spirit of God and ready to minister in their churches. I had heard people remark that this Bible school would not work, that it had been tried in Haiti before with negative results. But, when God gives you a vision and directions, do not listen to the naysayers and those who try to discourage you and make you doubt. Keep your eyes on the vision, and watch **God** bring it to pass!

May 2012 Bible School graduates with teachers

CHAPTER 16

Disasters: A Way of Life for Haitians

They sow the wind and reap the whirlwind. Hosea 8:7 (NIV)

IVING ON AN island in the Caribbean, it is inevitable that hurricanes and tropical storms will come your way. In the past 36 years in Haiti, we have been through many of these tropical storms and hurricanes—some minor and some major. But, since 2003 alone, we have had tropical storms or hurricanes in 2004, 2005, 2006, 2007, and 2008. Along with these storms or hurricanes, we have had floods in 2003 (twice), 2006, 2007, and 2008.

Just when you begin to feel you are making some progress, Satan tries to convince you that you aren't. In August 1980, Hurricane Allen, with a category five status, came roaring by Haiti with sustaining winds of up to 190 mph. Hurricane Allen first moved through the Atlantic Ocean, then the Caribbean Sea, and the Gulf of Mexico before making landfall near the US/Mexico border. At the peak of its strength, Hurricane Allen tore through Haiti.[5]

In my August 23, 1980, newsletter sent to our supporters, I wrote the following words:

> I have just finished this week making a survey of each of the churches and schools that we have. There was much damage to the roofs on the buildings of three of our churches: Blanchard, Boutin, and Robin. The six-inch building blocks were blown completely out of place on the walls. Doors will have to be replaced along with some windows. Benches were torn apart by the strong winds. We had an outstation that was a branch of the Robin church that was completely wiped out. Many homes of our people were destroyed. Our people lost what little they had, and the crops in the mountains were destroyed. I don't think my heart was ever so broken as we looked at the damage and the loss of the people. It will take about $20,000 to make repairs on our buildings alone. And this doesn't include any of the losses our people suffered.

I went on to tell my readers about a trip I took in President Duvalier's helicopter:

> Yesterday, I took a trip to the south of the island in the President's helicopter to check on the status of the people in the mountains. President Duvalier's sister, who is director of "Operation Combite," asked if I would go along on this mission with several others to see what we could do to help out.

> This remote area has no roads, and the helicopter pilot had trouble finding a place to land close to the village

in the mountains. The pilot flew back and forth across four mountain ranges trying to find a place to land and finally landed on a small patch of ground on top of one of the mountains. From the top of mountain, it was a five-mile trek to the village of Tête Beouf. If we wanted to fly back with him, we had to be back at the top of the mountain by a certain time, as he could not fly late in the afternoon with the clouds covering the mountains. As it turned out, we did not make it back to the designated spot on the mountain in time, and he left the group in the mountains to spend the night.

During our stay in that small village, many of the people came to us and said, "Pastor, can't you do just a little something for us?" Some of them had lost their homes and their gardens, which were the source of food and income; and some had lost all their possessions. Many had lost their lives, and in some cases, whole families were wiped out.

That evening, the people of the village came together to roast coffee beans, pound them up, and make coffee for our group to drink. I can still smell that delicious aroma of roasting coffee beans boiling over the open fire. For our dinner, the villagers boiled plantain bananas and yams they had dug up from the roots where they grew. Breakfast the next morning was roasted corn and more delicious coffee. They squeezed fresh oranges and made juice with grapefruit mixed in. We all knew these villagers had sacrificed and had given us the best they had, and we were thankful for it.

There were ten of us who were flying out to check on different villages, and there were ten of us who slept together in a room that was no bigger than 10 ft. x 10 ft. We weren't comfortable sleeping on the floor of that dark hut with bugs and spiders biting us and the heat feeling like it was going to suffocate us. When it started pouring rain later on in the evening, we became wet as the winds that blew the rain inside the hut. The rain had brought in a cold front and by this time it was too cold to do much sleeping. We all braved it out because we knew this would soon pass, and we would get to go back to our comfortable homes. I was so broken by the suffering of these poor people I couldn't help but think, "*Does anybody really, truly care about these dear people and their suffering?*"

I ended my newsletter by saying:

> It is not the time to feel sorry for ourselves, for there is much to do. Repairs will have to be made immediately as schools will be opening up in October. Our emergency fund is empty, and we need your help. I ask you, my dear friends, DO YOU REALLY CARE? Yes, I believe I know you well enough to say that not only do you care, but that you will SACRIFICE and GIVE to rebuild and help the people of Haiti at this time of great need. We cannot do anything until we hear from you!

Many of our supporters responded to our plea, and we did what we could to help these gracious people.

In 2008, we had four tropical storms that killed about 800 people. One tropical storm named Noel was particularly destructive at a time when our warehouse was almost empty. Many of our people lost their homes and possessions and their businesses. In a newsletter and through IMO's grapevine, we called on help from all our supporters.

And you answered with an abundance of supplies from mattresses to linens and five containers of food brought in to our headquarters in Clendenin by churches all over the United States.

And today, as I am writing this chapter, we have just had a tornado pass through Haiti. I have water all over my office, and so far, I don't know the extent of the damage anywhere else. I have never seen wind like this before, not even in all the hurricanes I have been through. Our phone is out, but the internet is back on. With all that has been happening recently, it looks like someone is angry at Haiti. Nevertheless, we are in revival here at Delmas, and Pastor Joe said they had a great meeting at Paillant. A blind lady was healed, and a person who had not walked by herself in years was healed instantly by the power of God. In four days, 38 people have come to know Christ and have given their lives to Him.

In Haiti, we have learned to live with a prayer on our lips. We pray about the big things like hurricanes and tropical storms, but we pray about little things too. We have to. We just don't have the resources to get ourselves out of situations like people do in other parts of the world. For example, over the years, our vehicles have broken down more times than I can remember. The roads in Haiti are very hard on vehicles. Actually, it is the lack of roads in Haiti that is the hardest on vehicles. Very few are paved, and the ones that are paved have so many washed out ruts by heavy rains that it is a rough ride to anywhere you go.

One day, several years ago, I had trouble with our Ford pickup truck. It just stopped on me in the middle of a busy road. Now, I consider myself a pretty good backyard mechanic, but I fiddled with that engine for about 30 minutes, with no success of getting it to turn over. Cars were blowing their horns at me to get out of their way, and the sweat was pouring off me like water running down a mountain stream. I was getting frustrated with the whole scene. So, I just got out of the truck and stood in front of it with my eyes closed and prayed in the name of Jesus that the trouble would go away. I put the air cleaner cover back on, closed the hood, and climbed back in the truck. It started right up! I shouted and praised the Lord all the way home. I dare anyone to tell me God does not care about all the little things that go on in our lives.

Yes, we do depend on God for everything simply because He has shown Himself dependable. We are always aware that all we have and all that we are come only from Him. The longer we serve Him, the more heavily we lean upon Him for not only physical needs but the more important emotional and spiritual needs too.

During those early days, we didn't have very many supporters, and times were very lean. This same scene has been repeated many times over during our stay in Haiti. Yet, somehow, the Lord always makes a way to provide what is needed. With the help of each person who supports our ministry, we rebuild, feed the hungry, and give help to as many families as we can that have suffered losses.

In the next chapters, I will tell you some of the things Joyce and I went through where we not only leaned on God, but He had to reach down, pick us up, and carry us through each day.

Through all the physical and emotional storms of life we experience here in Haiti, God provides and sustains us. Our supporters never fail to respond to our pleas and our cries. Our supporters always come through and help us move forward by the grace of God. When the response to disasters is so overwhelmingly good, all I can do is stand up and cry out, "LOOK WHAT THE LORD HAS DONE!"

CHAPTER 17

Evangelism: The Key To It All

. . . Take your sickle and reap, because the time to reap has come, for the harvest of the earth is ripe. Revelation 14:15 (NIV)

HEN JESUS PASSED through Samaria on His way back to Galilee one day, He paused for a rest near the plot of ground Jacob had given to his son Joseph. Jesus was by Himself, since His disciples had gone into the town to buy some food. Tired, hungry, and thirsty, Jesus sat down beside a well, known in the area as Jacob's well simply because it had been the well of Jacob's family. Shortly, a Samaritan woman came to draw water. As she began to lower her bucket into the well, Jesus asked her to give Him a drink. Astounded that a Jew would ask a Samaritan for anything since Jews despised and looked down upon the lowly Samaritans, she replied, "How can you ask me for a drink?" (John 4:9, NIV).

Jesus answered her, "If you knew the gift of God and who it is that asks you for a drink, you would have asked him and he would have given you living water" (John 4:10, NIV). Jesus went on to explain to her that, "Everyone who drinks this water will be thirsty again, but whoever drinks the water I give them will never thirst. Indeed, the water I give them will become in them a spring of water welling up to eternal life" (John 4:13-14, NIV).

IMO's mission in Haiti is to tell the Haitians about that spring of living water that can never run out! Since we have been in Haiti, we have dug over 40 wells to provide clean water for communities who had no water supply. But, digging wells, as important as that may be, is not our main mission to the people of Haiti. This is something we do to show Christ's love for them. Our main goal, and it has always been our foremost and most important goal, is to share the Gospel of Jesus Christ to the Haitians. Do not misunderstand. It is important to provide food, clothing, and water to those without, because when someone is really starving, naked, or thirsting for water, and all we offer them are words, they really do not pay much attention to us. On the other hand, if physical comforts are all we can offer them, then all we are doing is making them more comfortable temporarily. But if we can show them how to have springs of living water through Jesus Christ, we not only give them temporary comfort but eternal comfort as well.

According to the 2011 *CIA World Factbook*, there are more than 9.8 million people who live in Haiti—a country with only 10,000 square miles, mostly mountainous terrain. Can you imagine putting that many people in the state of Maryland, which is slightly smaller than Haiti? These statistics makes Haiti one of the most densely populated countries in the western hemisphere. Every major city is teeming with people everywhere—sidewalk to sidewalk, nothing but people. And according to Todd Johnson, director of the Center for the Study of Global Christianity at Gordon-Conwell Theological Seminary, throughout these major cities, there are over 1,700 career missionaries coming from many different denominations from all over the world because Haiti is a magnet for Christian ministries.[6] Several hundred additional missionaries travel to Haiti each year for short-term trips of a week or two at a time to provide aid and support to the career missionaries. Sometimes in the cities, you see missionary posts on top of one another.

Even with all this missionary activity going on in the major cities, there are still numerous providences with many thousands of people in the outskirts of the cities, tucked far away in the mountainous regions, who have never heard the Gospel of Christ. My heart is for evangelizing *all* of the country, not just the major cities. We *must* tell everyone about those springs of living water.

It is impossible to get the true religious picture of Haiti unless you travel to these remote providences. We have built churches in areas like Bois Chadeque in southeast Haiti, Rac Bois near Côtes-de-Fer in south Haiti, and Jean-Rabel in northwest Haiti. From our headquarters in Delmas, it takes about eight hours, give or take an hour or two, to reach any of these places—that is if the roads are not washed out. In addition, we have built churches at Fort-Liberté, Mapou, and Ferrier in the northeast section of Haiti and Thomonde and Hinche in the central plateau. All in all, IMO has built 45 permanent churches and 207 brush arbors or outstations throughout Haiti. Many of these churches are so remote that the roads leading up to the church are almost non-existent. And when an almost non-existent road ends, and all that is before you is a dirt path, you still have to travel by animal or foot to get to the actual church.

Who in their right mind wants to pastor a church or be a missionary in such a far out providence where electricity is unheard of and running water only comes when it rains? I knew the answer; we must train the Haitian people to become pastors, pastors who could reach these precious people in these far outlying regions of Haiti— Haitian pastors who could evangelize other Haitians! Evangelism is the key to it all.

Bible School students receiving certificates of completion for their second year. After three years, they receive graduation diplomas.

CHAPTER 18

Training Pastors: The Key to Evangelism

As long as the earth endures, seedtime and harvest,
cold and heat, summer and winter, day and night
will never cease. Genesis 8:22 (NIV)

I FIRMLY BELIEVE THAT *training Haitian pastors is the key to evangelizing all the country of Haiti, not just sending in more missionaries from other countries!*

Hundreds and thousands of precious people who live in the remote providences of Haiti need to hear the Gospel of Christ and how it can change their lives both here on earth and for eternity. Our vision is for our Bible school to train people from these remote areas who are called to be pastors and laymen. We know that when they return to their hometowns and families, they will teach others in their villages about Christ.

Just recently, we installed a new pastor, David Toussaint, at our

Saint-Marc church located on the western coast in central Haiti. We first met David at our Perisse school where he was a student. When he graduated, he felt God's call on his life, and he became a student in our Bible college. After graduating from Bible college, he returned to his hometown of Perisse and began teaching in our elementary school there. He also attended Eglise, IMO's church at Perisse, and eventually, David became the director of the Perisse school. It is so rewarding to see these young Haitian men and women develop into godly men and women who teach others about Christ.

When pastors and laypeople are trained and established in a church, we begin holding crusades and revivals in their areas. Each year, throughout the island, we hold 12 crusades—one crusade a month lasting three to four days. Every month, the location changes, as our goal is to reach out and evangelize the whole island of Haiti.

Holding a crusade is no easy task; there are many preparations that must be done in order to have a successful crusade. We have a team of seven or eight pastors from our Haitian churches that we send to help with the crusade and to preach during the crusade. The first thing the team must do is to secure permission from the mayor of the city to hold the crusade. Next, the team must contact the local police to let them know the crusade is coming to town. The police are very instrumental in keeping the crowd under control, for you never know what type of characters may show up at a crusade. The local IMO pastor is contacted, and his job is to contact other churches in the area and ask them to join in and be part of the crusade. Our goal for the crusades is to never promote IMO or us but to lift up and glorify Jesus Christ. And when Christ is lifted up, He draws in the crowds. Many people are saved during this time.

Regardless of where the crusade is held, our team of pastors must bring all the supplies needed for the crusade. Items taken to each crusade site include a generator for power, a 4,000-watt light, and all the sound equipment and musical instruments. We usually have about four or five musicians and seven or eight pastors to preach. We are housed in a church or school building, and we bring army cots to sleep on at night. We also take along all the food that will be needed to feed all the workers. There is one thing we can always count on wherever we go: mosquitoes! All we can do is bathe in insect repellant and pray. Sometimes we think we hear those mosquitoes singing, *"Nothing but the Blood!"*

Depending upon what God lays on our hearts, every year a particular theme is promoted throughout each crusade. That theme will culminates into the major theme of the big Haitian Convention held in January. This same theme is carried through to our seminars for pastors held each year in the spring and fall. One year, our united theme was "Have you received the baptism since you believed?" This theme is important because we believe that being filled with the baptism of the Holy Spirit is vital in a believer's life. Another year it was "Don't Hold Back, It's Time to Stretch." In Isaiah 54: 1-2, Isaiah told the barren woman to "shout for joy," and "enlarge the place of your tent, stretch your tent curtains wide, do not hold back; lengthen your cords, strengthen your stakes." Likewise, we firmly believe our ministry is getting ready to break forth on the right hand and on the left hand. Regardless of what theme is chosen, we carry it throughout the whole year in order to educate, unite, and strengthen our congregations, workers, and pastors.

I try to attend all the crusades, revivals, conventions, and seminars because evangelism is the key to all that IMO does. Without sharing the Gospel of Christ, IMO would become just another social organization providing temporary help. There are some discomforts involved, I admit. But, in Matthew 8:20, Jesus said that the birds have nests, but the Son of Man has no place to lay his head. It may be just an army cot, but God has always provided me with a place to lay my head.

Guest speaker Pastor Stewart Farley, front row far right, from Rhema Christian Center in Lewisburg, WV, with Haitian pastors in April 2012 Pastors Seminar. Gabriel Claxton, John's grandson, is standing directly behind Pastor Farley.

CHAPTER 19

The Miracle Results
of Evangelism

*When the harvest time approached, he sent his servants to
the tenants to collect his fruit. Matthew 21:34 (NIV)*

W E NEVER KNOW how God is going to work during one of
our crusades or in the many revivals held each year in our
churches; we just know *He will work*. We do our part by praying and
fasting, then we leave the results up to God. I would like to share with
you some of the miraculous results of evangelism we have witnessed
throughout our years of ministry.

During the crusades and revivals, there are many demon-possessed
people wanting us to pray for them. Although Roman Catholicism is
the official religion of Haiti, the majority of Haitians believe in and
practice at least some aspects of voodoo. Most voodooists believe
that voodoo and Christianity can coexist, but the Bible teaches us
this is not true. Educating new believers that God and Satan cannot

live in the same spiritual and physical body is a daunting task to such a culture steeped in centuries of "family traditions." It is only through the power and grace of God that any Haitian can come out victoriously in the battle against voodoo. I do not want to expound further on the religion of voodoo, but I need to say that the widely-believed system of voodoo lends itself to demon possession. Therefore, when this happens, and all the evil that comes along with it begins to destroy an individual's life, as a last resort, that person is brought to one of our crusades or revivals for prayer for deliverance.

At Chambrun, in an open-air crusade with some of our Bible students, there was a young girl who came to the altar for prayer. It was evident she was demon-possessed by her wild eyes, disheveled appearance, her snarling and clawing, and the extremely abnormal way she was acting. I prayed for her about five minutes, but she continued her snarling and grabbing at all of us who were praying for her. We continued to pray for her, and soon, God set her free and gave her peace. Those whom God has set free are free indeed!

In a crusade at Paillant, there was a woman who had caused a lot of disruptions during the night services. It was obvious that she was demon-possessed. Her dirty hair had bits and pieces of rags that the voodoo doctor had tied to her scalp to ward off evil spirits along with various kinds of junk hanging all over her body for protection. By Sunday morning, she was throwing things at the altar and yelling throughout the service. I told the leaders that the devil had to be cast out of her for she was disturbing everyone with her antics. We all got together and restrained her and began praying for her.

Let me say something here. Before you can cast out a demon, you always pray and cover yourself with the blood of Jesus. The devil hates the very mention of the blood of Jesus. You also need to know that the person wants that demon to leave. I asked the woman if she wanted to be set free of the demon, and she said, "Yes, but the voodoo doctor told me I will never be free." I told her she could be set free only by the grace and power of God. I then had her say, "I accept Jesus and his precious blood who set me free."

Before casting out demons, you have to prepare yourself for a pretty sneaky devil. If you are not careful, he can con you into thinking he has left the person who is possessed. But the devil knows and we know that all power in heaven and earth has been given to Christ, and before He ascended to heaven, He gave that power to the Christians who were the body of Christ. He instructed us that all we had to do was ask in His name and He would do it. When we tell the devil "in Jesus' Name," he has to leave—did you get that? *He has to leave!*

We continued praying for this lady, and shortly, a peace came over her. The first thing she started doing was to pull out all the bits of rags on her hair and to wipe off all the goo that was on her body. Today, she is working in the church and doing a faithful job. She was set free by the power of Jesus Christ. *Hallelujah!*

We do more than pray for the demon-possessed at our crusades. Sickness and disease is widespread throughout Haiti due to poverty, the unsanitary conditions that exist everywhere, and the lack of medical services. During a crusade at Cotin, the leaders felt led of the Lord to designate Thursday night as a "Praying for the Sick" night. Even though we always pray for the sick during a crusade, I can't ever remember designating a specific night in which to do so; nor have we done it since. But this particular night in Cotin, in an open field with about 150 people sitting on benches from the church, we began praying for the sick. Since we had announced to the community that we were going to pray for the sick this night, we had people lined up in the aisles waiting for prayer. There were three lines of people from the front to the back.

We began walking through each line praying for each person. We had gone about a fourth of way back on one line when we saw a woman who had been deaf from birth. She was 67 years old and had never heard a word in her life. We began praying for her. Immediately, God opened her ears, and she could hear! When she realized she could hear, she started spinning around in happiness, running through the field praising God. All the people were amazed. They knew this wasn't some trick or fancy setup. Everyone knows everybody in these areas, and the people all knew this woman had never been able to hear. Now she could hear, and the people knew they had just witnessed a miracle! And God was not finished amazing the people for the night.

We continued praying for the people standing in lines. About three-fourths of the way through one line, we saw a woman holding a small girl about five or six years old. I asked the lady what was wrong with the child. She explained that the little girl had never walked. I asked her why the little girl had never walked, and she just replied, "Because she can't."

I thought, "Well, let's just see." So, I asked the woman to set the little girl down on the ground. When the little girl was placed on the ground, her whole body became limp as a rag doll. It was as though she had no spine to prop up her frame. I prayed for her, and nothing happened immediately. And then, suddenly the Spirit of the Lord quickened her! Do you remember the story in Acts when Peter and John went to the temple to pray in the ninth hour of the day? They met a man at the temple who was begging for money, but Peter and John told him, "Silver or gold I do not have, but what I do have I give you. In the name of Jesus Christ of Nazareth, walk" (Acts 3:6, NIV). Peter took him by the hand and immediately his feet and ankles received strength.

Let me tell you that the same thing happened to that little girl! I reached down, took her arms, and lifted her up so that her feet were on the floor. She stood there trembling for a few seconds, looking like a newborn fawn trying to get the feel of its legs beneath its body. With her hand in mine, I walked with her across the front rows of benches three times back and forth. When I let go of her hand, she took off running! I'll never forget that miracle. But wait, that's not the best part of this story.

I truly believe God does not do miracles like these just to amaze people. When this crusade was over the following Sunday, one of the voodoo priests in that area came to the pastor of the Cotin church. The priest told him that on the night the woman and the little girl were healed, he had been standing way off in the shadows in a small hut where no one could see him. No one knew he was there listening to the service. He said, "I saw the woman and saw the little girl healed, and I said their God is the real God! I accepted the Lord right then."

The ex-voodoo priest went on to say that the next morning after the service, he gathered all of his family together, which included his wife, children, and all of his cousins, aunts, and uncles. There were 40 people who accepted Christ that morning because of what that voodoo priest had witnessed.

Miracles are important because God desires to manifest Himself. These signs are not to the believer, but to the unbeliever so that he may believe. I have found the Haitians are open to God's revealing Himself; they want this, therefore, they are able to believe He will reveal Himself in a miracle. They have not been influenced by all the religious writings of today that say God quit revealing Himself after the Bible was written.

Another way we promote evangelism is by having revivals at our churches. Most of IMO's churches have a couple revivals a year. We have churches that will take their people to other IMO locations to help hold revivals. Some of the greatest results are in the outstation brush arbor meetings. Many of the people have simple, childlike faith that is the breeding ground for God's presence to be made known. God honors faith. Hundreds come to Christ each year just because we take the time to reach out to those precious souls in the remote areas.

Before living in Haiti permanently, there was one revival I attended during one of my first trips there. The revival was held at Lascahobas, a town up in the central plateau of the country next to the eastern border. I preached at the morning service. I was getting into my pickup ready to leave, when I saw a blind girl in the middle of the road. Some of the people from the church brought her to me and asked me to pray for her. So I did. And God opened her eyes—just like that! Boy, was I surprised. I was new to the mission field, and honestly, I had not seen a lot of miracles at that time. But I could see that God was confirming to me, then, what He wanted to do in my ministry if I would obey and do His will.

There was another revival at Fort-Liberté. At the end of the Thursday night service, when the invitation was given for those who wanted to be saved, a young blind girl came up to the altar. She wanted to give her life to Jesus. When she prayed the prayer of repentance, God just opened her blind eyes, and she could see immediately. No one had even prayed for her to be healed. God healed her because He wanted to and could. That Sunday afternoon, I had the privilege of baptizing her in the Atlantic Ocean.

We have seen miracles even if there are no revivals or crusades taking place. One of my favorites—if there is such a thing as a favorite miracle—is one that happened when Pastor Stewart Farley and a group of men from Rhema Christian Center in Fairlea, West Virginia, were visiting IMO to put a new roof on the old Boutin school.

Papa Joey, a beloved brother in Christ who had sold us the land to build our first school and church at Boutin, had suffered a stroke. That Sunday morning in Boutin, before the church service, I told Pastor Stewart that we needed to go pray for Papa Joey. When we entered his home, he was so still and lifeless and hardly breathing at all. His whole left side—his arm, leg, and face—was paralyzed. He had no movement on that side at all. We prayed for him and left to go attend church.

When the service was finished, I felt led to go back and pray for Papa Joey again. I asked all of the members of the congregation, who really believed in their hearts that God was going to heal Papa Joey, to come with me. I didn't want any halfway believers along hindering God's work. About 15 people went to Papa Joey's home with Pastor Stewart and me. When we all entered his home, he sat up, and we got a little reaction from him. We prayed for him, and I told him that Pastor Stewart and his group of men were going to install the round roof on the church this week, and that he needed to be well enough to be there and help us. I let him know that I expected him to be up and moving and putting his faith in action. We left Papa Joey's home, and the next Wednesday, we headed back to Boutin to install the church roof.

When we began working on the roof, Papa Joey's family brought him out to the churchyard and sat him in a chair so he could see the work we were doing. He watched us all day; then on Thursday, they brought him out again to watch the men work. He watched us again all day. When we arrived Friday, we didn't see Papa Joey. Concerned about him, we asked his son, Joe, where he was.

"Oh, he'll be along soon," said Joe.

And sure enough, in about half an hour, here comes Papa Joey walking across the field to the church all by himself, walking as good as I could walk. As he walked, he had no limp, and the arm that had been paralyzed was raised toward the sky praising God for healing him. God had certainly touched and healed Papa Joey, and he lived a healthy life for many years after his stroke.

Have I mentioned how much I love seeing God work in the lives of these Haitian people?

Pastor John praying for a young man at IMO's Desmaret Church in Piallant, Haiti, in the mountain area, approximately 75 miles south of Port-au-Prince.

During the past 36 years, we have seen the lame walk, the blind receive their sight, growths and tumors disappear, legs made straight, cancers fall off, and deaf folks hear. Jesus said He would confirm His Word with signs and wonders. God does these miracles so the world can see that Christ is His Son, the Son who came to save those who are lost. Our crusades are all about winning SOULS.

Whether it is holding a crusade, having a revival, conducting a seminar for pastors twice a year to continue our pastors' religious education, or organizing an annual convention, evangelism is part of our everyday schedule. And the best tool of evangelism is treating others the way Christ taught us. Our everyday living does more witnessing for Christ than all the words we can preach. To have a solid, daily, Christian witness, we have to be willing to spend time with God, getting to know what His will is for our lives every minute of every day. Satan wants nothing more than to keep us from getting to know God and our inheritance. The Lord wants us to get up close and personal with Him. He wants to develop a relationship with us that is better than anything else this world has to offer. And He wants us to tell others they can have this relationship also. God wants Christians who are faithful to spend time on their knees getting to know what His will is and eager to carry out His will.

Evangelizing the Haitians burns in my heart. God put that desire in my heart many years ago, and today, it burns stronger and hotter than it ever has before. And the most wonderful miracle of all is that God has never failed in giving me the tools and means in which to evangelize the nation of Haiti.

CHAPTER 20

Meet Some of Our Adopted Families

The LORD will indeed give what is good, and our land will yield its harvest. Psalm 85:12 (NIV)

T OUR HEADQUARTERS, Joyce and I begin each day having devotions with our leaders and workers. On one particular day, I had Edner, our Director of Education, read John 13, where Jesus took the towel and washed the disciples' feet, showing that He came to serve and to save, not to be served. When Edner was finished reading, I had Estime, the guardian, the lowest paid employee on the compound, sit in a chair in front of the group who had assembled for the devotions. Panyel placed a bowl of water and a towel beside the chair, and I went over and removed Estime's shoes and socks. Gently and lovingly I washed off his feet, and in front of the staff who had gathered that morning for devotions, I prayed for his needs and those of his family.

It was important to me to let our people know that Joyce and I came to Haiti to serve them. We wanted our workers to know we are not above anyone here, and that is the way every Christian should feel. Our workers and leaders were so moved and touched by this one simple deed that they all cried. I think they got our message when they saw it in action, and it was much more effective than all the words I could have preached to them. These workers and leaders are our adopted family. I pray that wc will be more like Jesus every day that we live.

Joseph Fils Constant

Pastor Joe is a quiet man with a very expressional face when he talks about the things he loves the most. His eyes are intense, and the words he speaks come from his heart. His smile has a hint of mischief. It's a teasing smile. As he speaks, he illustrates his words with his hands.

> I am 53 years old, and I am the pastor of the Boutin Church. Since I pastor the church, I live on the property at Boutin in a wonderful house IMO has built for me. My wife's name is Marie Oramene, and we have eight children—four boys and four girls.
>
> When I was 12 years old, I became a student at Boutin in the very first school IMO built. My father, Papa Joey, sold the school and church property to Pastor John in 1976. My father was a farmer who worked in a garden, and on the streets of Port-au-Prince, my mother sold the produce from our garden. After the school and church were built, my father became the caretaker of the property, and my mother became a cook for the school. I have two brothers and one sister.

As a child, I was very blessed to have a Christian father and mother who always took me to church and Sunday School. It was a special blessing the day my father allowed Pastor John to preach from his front porch and tell the community of Boutin about Jesus Christ.

In 1984, I felt the call of God to become a pastor. Before then, I taught Sunday School and was a schoolteacher for five years at our school in Boutin, and in 1984, I became the principal at Boutin. In 1988, after Bible college I became the pastor of our church at Boutin.

God has truly blessed our ministry at Boutin. One thing I have learned about God is: He wants to heal the sick. One of the ladies in my congregation had a little girl who was very sick. The child had been taken to a doctor, but the doctor told her mother that she needed to go to the hospital because she was too sick for him to help her. The mother brought the little girl to our medical clinic at Boutin. On this particular clinic day, Mme. Pastor Joyce had brought with her some missionary friends. When Mme. Pastor saw the little girl and how sick she was, she called on her missionary friends and me to pray for her. After we all prayed, Mme. Pastor gave the little girl some medicine and sent her home. God healed that little girl, and she is now a grown up lady with a family in our church today.

God not only wants to heal the sick, He wants to raise the dead! Here at Boutin we were hosting one of IMO's yearly conventions. During the morning service, a small baby boy died. I was preaching in the pulpit when I noticed some commotion in the back of the church. I stopped my preaching and went to stop the mother of the dead baby who was going out the back door of the church. The mother had given the dead baby to a lady friend to keep while she was going home to tell her husband what had happened to the child. The lady friend tried to leave the service with the baby, but I reached for the baby and cradled him in my arms. I began praying for this child not knowing anything except my God was capable of anything, and, right then, we needed a miracle. When the mother returned with the husband to get the baby, the baby boy was sitting beside the lady friend and was eating some food. That morning, there was no doubt in our minds that God had blessed us with an unbelievable miracle!

My heart's desire is to teach my congregation the true Word of God. I want to challenge them to serve God faithfully and not let the natural things of this world take their minds off their focus on God.

Sometimes in life, you find yourself searching for something, and that search becomes a big trial for you. When I was young, I kept searching for something, and I did not even know what I was looking for. When Pastor John and Mme. Pastor Joyce came into my life, they showed me what I had been missing in my life and that was Jesus Christ and my salvation. Pastor John and Mme. Pastor Joyce have not only been spiritual parents to me but also physical parents. Pastor John and Mme. Pastor Joyce are like a good gift, because they invested their time and money in my life. If I have knowledge, it is because of them. I honestly do not know what type of life I would be living today if it were not for them. For this and all the many things they have done for me, I will always love them and never forget their acts of unselfishness and sacrifice.

Edner Blanc

One glance at Edner and you know here is someone you would never be able to put anything over on. Besides being 6 ft. 2 in. and larger than the average Haitian, he has that look about him that tells you, "Been there, done that" and "you can't fool me!" Edner is IMO's official translator since he has worked hard learning to speak the English language. When Haitian pastors preach at IMO's yearly convention in the states, Edner is the translator. He also translates for John in Haiti if it is ever necessary.

I am 45 year old, and I have been the pastor of the church at Robin since 1988. My wife's name is Acela, and we have three children—one boy and two girls.

When I was a student at IMO's school at Blanchard, sometimes I went to school, and sometimes I stayed home. I always liked to do whatever I wanted to. My father and mother were never married, and I spent most of my time at my father's house. I had some stepbrothers that were my father's children, but my mother had only me. Mom sold items on the streets of Port-au-Prince to earn her living.

I took advantage of the educational opportunities that were given to me growing up, and I attended IMO's school, Blanchard II, in École. When I was about 21 years of age, I was offered a teaching position at one of IMO's school. Let me tell you that, all my life, I have had problems with those in authority. So, it was no surprise to my friends and family when I began having difficulties with the school's principal. Many people thought I was rude and arrogant, because I *was* rude and arrogant! After having worked with me and warning me, which netted no results, Pastor John fired me from my school teaching job.

Shortly after being fired, Pastor John called me to come to his office. He told me he had been praying for me, and he thought the best thing for me to do was to go to Bible school. He told me, "The Bible school will change your life."

"Big promise," I thought. I explained to him that I could not go to Bible school because I had a family to support and I had to work. "Who will take care of my family?" I asked him.

Pastor John told me, "God will take care of your family." Of course, Pastor John knew God would use **him** to help take care of us!

I agreed to go to Bible school, and Pastor John and IMO helped me all they could. In that one year at Bible school, my life was completely changed! Through learning the true Word of God presented by the godly teachers at the Bible school, for the first time in my life, I truly repented and dedicated my life to God. In the past, I had always gone to church because Mama did, and she expected me to go. I tried to do all the things that people expected me to do, but I never really had any true commitment. I guess I was trying to get to heaven on Mama's religion.

After only one year at Bible school, the teachers saw the change in me, and Pastor John also noticed how my attitude was different. It was all because I truly committed my life to Christ at the Bible school. At that time, we only had a two-year Bible school. Because of the drastic changes the Bible school had made in me, Pastor John was now asking me to teach some classes to the first year students. Then in 1988, I became the pastor of the church at Robin, where I am still ministering today.

I do not have the words to express how much I love and appreciate Pastor John and Mme. Pastor Joyce. My friends and family used to tell me that because of my attitude, I would never become anything or be successful. Because of the influence of Pastor John and Mme. Pastor Joyce, my life has been changed so much that everyone can now see that, through Christ, I have become someone my family is proud to acknowledge. And it is all because nothing is too hard for the God I serve!

My dream and vision for my congregation is to take them to a higher level with God than they have ever been before. I don't want any of my congregation's feet to stay planted on the ground but to be always climbing the mountains, reaching toward impossible heights!

Feriel Duverus (Panyel)

Panyel has gentle eyes. There is depth and wisdom behind those eyes that seem to see right into the inner chamber of your heart. Panyel's story is one that epitomizes the proverb that says, "If you are faithful in the small things, you will be ruler over greater things." From a "Gate Keeper" to a "Key Keeper"—that is our beloved Panyel, who has proven and continues to prove himself a worthy servant of the Lord.

I am 55 years of age and have been employed by Pastor John and Mme. Pastor Joyce since 1977, shortly after they came to Haiti to live on a permanent basis. I have three sons.

I was a very young man when I first came to work for Pastor John as a gatekeeper in Mariane, where Pastor John worked at the time. I had been saved at the age of nine in our small Baptist Church at Côtes-de-Fer, which is located in the southern part of Haiti. I had some cousins who were always trying to find me a job, and they told me about the missionaries who were looking for someone to attend the gate at their mission guesthouse. It was a very small job, paying very little money, but it was an important one to me. I had gone to school for a few years, but I had to stop and go to work to help my parents support my large family of five brothers and four sisters.

I began working for Pastor John just to open and close a gate, but God gave me the knowledge to do many other things. I mowed grass, loaded the vehicles, and served as a handyman, learning all I possibly could about any job anyone was willing to teach me. After three months, I was trusted with keys to all the buildings.

When I first started out with Pastor John, I knew nothing—really nothing! But the more I worked alongside him and the more he taught me, the realization came to me that my head—my mind—was like a calculator or computer. God has given me the ability to learn quickly and grasp the workings of machinery, electricity, plumbing, and just about anything that goes into creating or building something. People sometimes ask me how I do it, and I say, "I just do it!" That's God.

Pastor John has invested many hours teaching me and showing me how to do all the things he learned growing up. I am grateful for all the knowledge he has imparted to me. Pastor John tells me that I am the first person he goes to when he needs to get a job done quickly. God has given me a creative mind, and I know in my heart it was God's plan to put me in Pastor John's life to be his helper.

I could write my own book about my relationship with Pastor John and Mme. Pastor Joyce. It would take several volumes to write about the experiences I have had, starting from my humble beginnings in Côtes-de-Fer to my job as second in command at IMO compound work. Even though Pastor John and I come from different backgrounds, we are one in the Spirit. I grew up and became a man under the guidance of Pastor John and Mme. Pastor Joyce.

Joubert Lamy

Joubert is our Co-Director General of all our IMO schools. He is currently over 129 teachers, 17 directors, and one inspector. His brother is Pastor Charles Lamy, who is pastor of our Delmas Church.

His sister, Caroline, works with Joyce in our offices. Without Joubert's influence, our schools would not be what they are today. Joubert's love for education has been the driving force in bringing them up to a higher level. Joubert is also a liaison between Pastor John and the governmental offices in Haiti. Whatever Joubert is needed to do, he is willing to do it.

I am 52 years old, and I have been working for IMO for 25 years. My wife's name is Josette, and we have three boys. I have a degree in accounting from a Haitian professional college. My father died when I was in the sixth grade, and Mom raised eight kids by selling food and items on the street. I went to a public Catholic School in Port-au-Prince. I was blessed to be raised in a Christian home and to have a mother who knew the power of love and the power of prayer. She also knew the power of disciplining all of us kids!

My first job with IMO was teaching at École IMO Delmas, and I was also a liaison between the school director and Pastor John and Mme. Pastor Joyce. When that school director left, I took his place. I was there about 15 years until I came to the headquarters in Delmas. There, I took a job being an inspector for all the schools. An inspector visits all the schools and sees that the teachers and directors are fulfilling their obligations to the Department of Education. After several years as an inspector, I was promoted to Co-Director General over all the teachers, directors, and inspectors. If any feedback is negative from an inspector, it is my job to work together with Pastor John to resolve the problem.

Meanwhile, we are working and striving to carry out plans to educate the country of Haiti. In some missions where you are hired as a teacher, the leaders want to have complete control of everything you do, and you must stay strictly under their guidelines. I am grateful for Pastor John and Mme. Pastor Joyce who give us the freedom to worship God and teach us to listen to the voice of God when we have decisions to make.

One year I went on a trip to Boston, Massachusetts, for two weeks to visit my brothers who are plumbers there. They were trying to get me and my family to move to Boston, where the quality of life is much, much better than in Haiti. I told them that I will work at IMO as long as Pastor John and Mme. Pastor are here.

I appreciate IMO and the work Pastor John and Mme. Pastor Joyce are doing in my beloved country. I count it a privilege to be working with them in accomplishing the goals God has given them. I want to work with them until they leave Haiti.

Front row, left to right: Joyce and John Hanson. Second row, left to right: Pastor Lamarre Lamy, Pastor of IMO Delmas Headquarters church; Pastor Joseph Fils Constant, Pastor of IMO's Boutin Church and Representant of IMO to Haitian Government; Feriel (Panyel) Duverus, Director of Operations, Delmas Central, for Construction; Joubert Lamy, Co-Director and Inspector of IMO Schools; Pastor and IMO Interpretor, Edner Blance, of IMO's Robin Church.

CHAPTER 21

The Kidnapping

A wicked person earns deceptive wages, but the one who sows righteousness reaps a sure reward. Proverbs 11:18 (NIV)

ONE DECEMBER MORNING in 2009, Joyce and I were preparing to head home to the States and were looking forward to being with our family for Christmas. On the evening before our departure, I received a phone call that changed our plans all together.

I was stunned beyond words when Maxo Duverus, who works at the headquarters at IMO and who is Panyel's (Feriel Duverus) brother, called telling me that Panyel and Elda had been kidnapped and were being held for ransom. It took a few moments for me to process this information. How was it possible that Panyel—who I trusted with everything, who has been with me from the beginning days of IMO, and whom no son could be loved more—had been kidnapped? And Elda—who has been a cook and housekeeper at our headquarters since the beginning—had been kidnapped with him. What must they be going through now? Are they still alive? Are they hurt? All these questions kept running through my frightened and troubled mind.

Maxo told me the kidnappers had made contact with him through Panyel's cell phone, and they were demanding $150,000 US dollars (Approximately $50,000 Haitian dollars) for their release. Panyel had given the kidnappers Maxo's number, knowing that he would contact me for help. He didn't want the kidnappers to know the organization for which he worked or they would have demanded more money.

The anger that I felt was indescribable. It was as if someone had physically tied up my hands and feet, and I was at the mercy of monsters. We had heard stories on television of all the kidnappings in Haiti, but to be honest with you, I just believed that Joyce and I and our staff were untouchable. A week prior to this, a small Haitian boy was kidnapped, and the kidnappers had demanded only $680 in US dollars for ransom money. But it might as well have been a million dollars, because the boy's family was too poor to raise even that amount. So, the kidnappers killed the little boy. That thought stayed before me. At this point, I was frightened and scared out of my mind!

I had to think quickly; what do I do? Notifying the police was not an option; I knew full well they would do nothing. I also knew beyond any doubt that if I didn't negotiate with the kidnappers, they probably wouldn't hesitate to kill Panyel and Elda and then go out and find someone else. It was up to me. As fearful as I was, I knew I served a God who would not let me down.

It was about 9:00 p.m. when we got the call from Maxo, so there was nothing I could do that night. I slept fitfully, but in the morning, as soon as I could, I called together some of our Haitian pastors for support and prayer. Also, I called Maxo, Panyel's brother, and a Haitian lawyer I had used before for some legal work, to come and be with me. I felt I needed all the help and support around me praying for God to give me wisdom and guidance on how to handle this horrible situation. We also called all our Haitian staff together to pray for Panyel's and Elda's safe return.

Periodically, the kidnappers called Maxo and demanded the ransom. Sometimes, when the kidnappers called demanding the money in exchange for Panyel and Elda, they would let Panyel talk to us to prove he was still alive. But mostly, they just demanded their money and threatened to kill Panyel and Elda if we did not pay.

Our negotiations continued for two and a half days. We would talk to the kidnappers and tell them what we could do, and they would say they would get back to us. Then, we all would pray. Negotiating and praying, negotiating and praying—for two and a half days. Those were the longest days of my life. Through each phone conversation with the kidnappers, the ransom demand decreased as we tried to convince them we could raise only a certain amount of money and any larger amount would be impossible. On the third day, all parties agreed that $2,500 US dollars (Approximately $1,500 Haitian dollars) was a fair price.

IMO was able to come up with all the money to pay this ransom demand! Then, the ransom money was given to the lawyer who had been helping us negotiate the "fair price." Around 3:00 p.m. that day, the lawyer was told by the kidnappers to meet them at a certain location, and he was also told to come alone or Panyel and Elda would be killed. The lawyer put the money in a sack and left to go where he had been instructed to take the money. Once the lawyer got to the appointed place, the kidnappers called and told him to go somewhere else. When he arrived at this second place, he got further instructions to go to yet another place. This cat-and-mouse game continued for about two hours until he finally met the kidnappers and turned over the ransom. The lawyer was told they would release Panyel and Elda when it became dark. For several long, stressful hours, the kidnappers had Panyel, Elda, and our money.

After three stressful days, Panyel and Elda were released at 9:00 p.m. to Maxo at the same place in which they were kidnapped. Previously, the police, though they had never been notified about the kidnapping, had found Panyel's Chevrolet pickup abandoned by the kidnappers and had towed it to their station yard. Maxo had intended to bring Panyel and Elda back to the compound, but I told Maxo to take them to their families first. I knew how anxious they would be to see them safe and unharmed.

Very early the next morning after his release, Panyel arrived at the compound and came directly to our apartment. He knocked on my door crying loudly, "I'm here. I'm here, Pastor John." When he saw me he came running across the room and jumped up in my arms and locked his legs around my belly, holding his arms tightly around my shoulders (Panyel is only 5 ft. 4 in. tall, and I am 6 ft. 2 in.). He held onto me like he would never let go. And then he sobbed like a little baby. He kept telling me "I knew you wouldn't leave me and go to the States, I knew you wouldn't leave me. God kept showing me your face and telling me you would still be here when I got freed."

You talk about shouting and praising the Lord! Panyel and I had our own little praise and worship service right in our living room. When we both finally settled down, I called all the staff together, and Panyel began to tell them the story of how they were kidnapped.

This is Panyel's story:

> Elda and I were on our way home after working at the IMO headquarters, when I remembered I was out of minutes on my cell telephone. [Elda lives just a few blocks from Panyel, and she rides to work with him every day.] I stopped at a store and bought some minutes. [In Haiti, all cell phones use prepaid minutes; there are no billing companies.]
>
> I got back in the pickup and drove for a few minutes until I found a place I could pull over and park. I began scratching off the numbers of the prepaid phone card to install them in my cell phone when something caused me to look up. That's when I saw

two guns pointed at Elda's head. Immediately, I saw another gun pointed at my head. The guys with the guns began demanding that we give them all our money. We told them that we only had about $6.00 between the two of us. That small amount didn't make the men very happy.

We were told to get out of the pickup and get into the back seat on the floor of the extended cab. They immediately made us put a hat over our heads, so it was hard to tell how many kidnappers there actually were. As near as we could tell there were four of them.

I don't think this was a planned kidnapping. We just stopped at the wrong time at the wrong place. Maybe they thought we were counting money when we pulled over to install the minutes on the phone. Even though we didn't think this was a planned kidnapping, the kidnappers had come prepared. They had guns that they kept aimed at us continuously, and they had the hats that went over the top of our heads. The only thing we could see was a little daylight at our chin level.

We drove in my pickup for what seemed like hours and hours. When the truck finally stopped, they made us get out. I could tell by the lay of the land that we were in a mountainous area. We walked and climbed up this mountain for hours. The terrain was so steep and rough at times, that we had to get on our hands and knees and crawl to make it up the hills. Our hats were never taken off our heads, and the climb was so terribly hard. I tried to help Elda. I could hear her cry out as she stumbled or fell, but they kept us separate. I felt someone's hand on me the whole time. I could hardly see anything at all because by this time, it was night. I truly felt helpless. I kept praying to God to keep us safe.

I had no idea where the men were taking us. Eventually, we came to a shack, and Elda and I were shoved into a small room about 4 ft. x 5 ft. and told to lay face down on the dirt floor of the room. Once we were secured in the room, a man took off our hats and put blindfolds over our eyes. All this was done at gunpoint.

A man brought us a bowl of soup water with bread to eat. We were not allowed to go outside the room, so we had to use the bathroom where we lay. We were not allowed to talk to each other or to the kidnappers. When the kidnappers disappeared, a guard was left in charge. Although I could never see him, I had the opportunity to reach out and touch his arm. It was a very small, boney arm. He didn't seem like a very large man at all. I got a chance to talk with him some, and I found out that he had been kidnapped by these very same men. Because he nor his family could come up with any money, they made him work for them keeping guard over this shack in the mountains whenever they had prisoners. When I could, I told him about the love of Jesus, how I had been set free from sin, and how God would and could do the same for him. It is amazing that no matter what your circumstances are, there is someone worse off than you are who needs God's love.

For two and a half days, we stayed in the small room blindfolded. The only other food they gave us was a bowl of rice. On the third day, the kidnappers returned at dark and took us out of the room. Fear gripped my heart. I didn't know if they were going to kill us or let us go. They put the hats back over our heads, and we began our decent down the mountain we had just climbed up three days ago.

Around 9:00 p.m. on the evening of the third day of our capture, we were taken back to the area where we had been kidnapped, and we were released.

After Panyel finished telling his story, he and I had another shouting and praise service, giving glory to God for his protection over our brother and sister in Christ. What a tremendous testimony of God's unlimited power and goodness this story was to our staff and to all of IMO's people as they all joined forces to pray and raise money for the ransom.

Because Elda had gotten sick during her time at the shack, it took a few weeks for her to recover her strength and return to work. Panyel returned to work in only a week. It was a horrible and frightening experience for both of them, but when Panyel shares his testimony with others, he smiles and says, "I serve a real God who takes care of His children, no matter what they go through."

CHAPTER 22

The Quake

If we have sown spiritual seed among you, is it too much if we reap a material harvest from you? 1 Corinthians 9:11 (NIV)

January 12, 2010, Tuesday, 5:00 p.m. EST
Day 1

JOYCE AND I had just entered our apartment on the third floor of our guest quarters and had sat down to rest, when we heard a noise from outside sounding like a thundering herd of freight trains. Immediately, we were thrown up in the air and then onto the floor, but the force didn't leave us there. We were blown around the room like dandelions in the wind. Tables, chairs, lamps, mirrors, knickknacks, and books came flying by us, coming from everywhere in the room, whipping around as though they had no weight at all. The building's vibrations were so powerful we couldn't stand up. Somehow, someway—and I really don't know how—I grabbed hold of Joyce and put her in a chair. I covered her with my body, because I knew the concrete ceiling and walls were going to collapse down upon us. Then we waited for the end.

A few long seconds later, the noise level lessened; I sensed the vibrations easing, and then ceasing altogether. It was total quiet for a second or two. The chaos had been going on for about a minute and a half, but it seemed like forever. Thoughts began to form quickly in my mind. Was there more to come? Was it safe to move yet? Was it safe if we didn't move? Can we make it out the door and down the three flights of steps before it happens again?

"We're alive! Praise the Lord! Let's go, Joyce!" I shouted, and quickly, we climbed over the battered furniture and broken glass and made our way to the front door. We cleared out a path of debris so we could open the front door. A cloud of dust thicker than pea soup met us as we stepped out onto the patio. Blindly and carefully, we descended the three floors of steep iron steps, coughing all the way as our lungs breathed in the large cloud of dust surrounding our compound.

We heard children crying and screaming as we came down the stairs. Where was the screaming coming from? The dust in the air was so thick we could hardly see our feet on the steps in front of us, and the cloud of powdered concrete in the air seemed to extend as high up as our eyes could see. Through the haze, we could see that our 12-foot wall behind our guest quarters had collapsed, and the two-story school building on the other side of the collapsed wall had caved in too. The crying and yelling were coming from children in that school. We reached the ground and saw a few of our workers, who had not yet gone home, standing in the yard. I told the workers to get to the school behind us and try to rescue those children.

Still dazed and confused, Joyce and I began checking out the buildings on the compound and were relieved that they were all still standing; they were damaged, but none had collapsed! Thank you, Lord! As we went from building to building, we watched the scenes of chaos unfolding before us as though we were bystanders watching the making of a disaster movie. Fortunately, none of the workers left on the compound were injured. As we went from room to room, we kept calling on the name of Jesus, over and over again, as we tried to make sense of this horrible event our eyes were witnessing. For fear of another tremor, we stayed in the buildings just long enough to make sure no one needed our help, but it was long enough to see the complete devastation of every room and everything in it. We were stunned and scared, and I kept telling Joyce everything was going to be all right. But, I don't think I believed my own words.

Shortly, our workers returned to the yard and gave us a report on the school children rescue. All 20 children were taken out of the collapsed school safely; some had cuts and broken limbs, but they were all safe. A two-story school building collapses and every child gets out safely? Wow! Praise your name, Jesus!

We then focused our attention on one of our Bible students coming through the front gate. He had terrible cuts on his head and legs from being hit by falling concrete blocks. His legs had already begun to swell. I knew those gashes would need to be cleaned and bandaged, and he would also need pain medicine. I headed to our pharmacy room on the bottom floor of our four-story guest and living quarters building. I pushed open the pharmacy door, and it budged a little, just enough for me to get in and see that everything inside was upside down and a complete mess. I quickly found some bandages, tape, and pain medicine among the scattered medical supplies, then I left abruptly as I began to feel the tremors shaking the building again. I crawled over things as I made my way back out of the shaking building.

We cleaned and doctored the student's wounds. By then, other people began coming in the front gate looking for help. For the rest of the evening, we made several more trips to the pharmacy to get medical supplies to treat the injured that came to us for help.

When nightfall came, we didn't feel safe going back to our

third-story apartment, so we spent the night in one of our one-story volunteer apartments. Sleep evaded us for the most part, and finally, when we were able to close both eyes, it was a stressful slumber. We kept thinking about what was happening to everyone outside our compound walls. By the screaming and hollering outside our walls all night long, we knew there were many others out there who were struggling to keep it all together and make sense of what had just happened.

So far, we had not been able to get word to our daughters that we were safe. We knew they must be anxiously waiting for us to call. Questions kept going over and over in our heads. Were all our workers and their families safe? How badly did the earthquake hit all our schools and churches? How long would it take before we could find out the answers to all these questions?

In the days to follow, we would discover that outside our compound walls, tons and tons of concrete rubble pounded the ground as buildings fell down all over the city of Port-au-Prince and its surrounding areas. If the buildings didn't come down on the first wave of tremors, the many subsequent tremors got them. Houses and businesses we had passed by hundreds of times had been reduced to a huge pile of concrete rubble, looking as though they had been demolished by a giant wrecking crane in one fell swoop!

For days, the screaming continued, and people kept running around looking for lost loved ones. When they discovered they were trapped inside a building, they went looking for someone to help get them out, but with little success.

We learned quickly that mass confusion was queen at this time and fear was her king. There was no doubt now, total chaos was in charge.

January 13, 2010, Wednesday
Day 2

For a split second when I first opened my eyes today, I wondered if the earthquake had been just a horrible nightmare. Immediately,

I knew I was not in my right bedroom. The earthquake had really happened. Where do I go from here? What do we do first? How do I fight this overpowering feeling of discouragement and be strong for all the people who need me? We are going to need so many things just to survive that my mind cannot comprehend it all. Our warehouse supplies are limited since we had given generously to our congregations during the Christmas season. How can just a few moments in time set us back 20 or 30 years in all that has been accomplished? My heart is crying tears.

January 14, 2010. Thursday
Day 3

There is no electricity, phones, or running water provided by the city's utility company. Today, we finally have internet service, only because we have generators here on the compound. And the most wonderful thing of all was we were able to get our Vonage phone system up and running and contact our two daughters, Cindy and Faithe. What a wonderful time that was as we talked and wept and praised God for sparing our lives. How great it was to be able to let them know we were safe. As our voices cracked with emotion trying to hold back the tears, we thought of all the thousands of people who would never be able to contact their loved ones again. I will never forget our phone reunion that day. Life is very precious, and oh, how quickly it can be taken away from you. But how can one truly understand how tenuous life is until something like this happens?

Our fuel is frighteningly low now, down to 170 gallons of diesel and no gasoline, as we had just put in a new order the day of the earthquake for 2,000 gallons of diesel and 1,500 gallons of gasoline. We have the money to purchase items, but there is no place open to buy food water, bread, or anything. *I have never felt so helpless in all my life!*

January 15, 2010, Friday
Day 4

Today, we made our way very carefully up the stairs and into our apartment and found all the furniture upside down and everything broken and scattered all over the place. All furniture cabinets and drawers along with all the built-in cabinets throughout the apartment had been emptied and their contents lay broken on the floor, so many material possessions destroyed or damaged beyond repair. Even though we lost many things, we were grateful we had not been hurt. As we stood there in the living room looking at the destruction, we couldn't help but think that over a period of time, we will be able to replace all these "things," but we knew we would never be able to replace one another. Joyce and I have been together now for over 50 years, and I thank God for every day we have been together. What a wonderful helpmate God provided for me!

As we searched through the debris, we loaded up the cans of food that were still good and a few plastic bottles of water that were undamaged. Every little bit was going to be important for survival in the days to come. We took these supplies to our one-room volunteer quarters and began the process of setting up our headquarters there. For the next three weeks, we used this one-room quarters as our base to begin the gigantic clean-up and repair tasks we had before us.

Before we could do anything, we had to assess all the damages and then prioritize the order in which we would make repairs and clean up messes. We went from building to building on the compound in a daze, still stunned by what had happened. Little by little, bits and pieces of information came to us through our grapevine network, but we could not travel to any of our churches or schools as the roads were still blocked by fallen concrete and were not passable. To further complicate traveling, people who had lost their homes had begun using the roads as makeshift homes because empty space was so scarce.

Most of the information we received was not good. We were dismayed to learn that one of our Bible school cooks, Paulette, had a daughter who was attending a vocational school in Port-au-Prince, and because of the earthquake, she was trapped under three floors of concrete and mangled steel. For four days, we prayed for her until she died at 10:00 p.m. the fourth night. We knew there was little we could do for Paulette as God was the only One who could heal her hurt now. What we didn't know was there would be many, many more of our loved ones who would go through this same hurt.

We have completely depleted our food supply, and water is running low. But I just talked to our friend and supporter, Steve Redford, from Branson, Missouri, who told me that he is flying his plane down here this weekend with a load of food, water, and medical supplies. He is flying into the Dominican Republic Airport and will make arrangements to have the supplies brought to us here. Thank you Lord, for men who are guided by You.

January 16, 2010, Saturday
Day 5

We went to the Port-au-Prince Airport to wait for Steve's arrival today. His face was a beautiful sight to behold as he arrived with the food and water and medical supplies from the States and, also, with more supplies he had purchased when he arrived in the Dominican Republic. In addition, he had arranged for 16,000 pounds of rice, beans and cooking oil to be brought to us by another plane that eventually had to make several trips to get all the supplies to us. We were able to give this food to our workers and their families. What a tremendous blessing we received today!

Finally, food and supplies are making their way here to Haiti by way of the Dominican Republic merchants and are available for the public to buy. We will start buying food and water for our workers and their families and try to help ease some of the pain they are going through.

January 17, 2010, Sunday Morning
Day 6

The crowd began gathering this morning at our Delmas Church in the compound long before it was service time. People had come to sing and praise the Lord they serve for protecting them from harm. Many of them had family members who were killed or injured, but here they were, praising and giving God the glory for keeping them safe. God is a good God. One thing you cannot do is steal the joy from a child of God. We go through tough times—and we are surely there now—but God will see us through this. He always has.

Thank God for our Vonage phone service! Using the Vonage phone, I did over 60 live phone interviews with TV and radio stations this past week throughout the United States in an effort to get the word out how desperately help is needed. In addition, I talked live with several church congregations in the States today. As my voice went out over the airways, I prayed that God would give these congregations compassion for the people in Haiti.

The more we get the word out, the more people are responding. Pastor Darrell Huffman, from New Life Church in Huntington, West Virginia, contacted a friend of his in the Dominican Republic, and his friend has purchased seven more tons of rice, beans, and cooking oil. God has already begun working out some of the many problems facing us. What a mighty God we serve. He is so faithful!

January 19, 2010, Tuesday
Day 8

For the past three days, we have been purchasing food, water, and building supplies for our people and, also, giving them cash so they can purchase the food and tents they need to survive. To date, we have given out or spent over $50,000. This is such a small amount compared to what is needed. But with this small amount, we have been able to help over 1,900 families totaling over 17,000 people living in tents, under bed sheets, and tarps in the streets. Over 400,000 Haitians have left the city to go try and find shelter in the country with family or just in the mountains. But that still leaves one and a half million people looking for food and shelter.

January 20, 2010, Wednesday
Day 9

There was another tremor measuring 6.0 on the Richter scale today. Eight days after the first one, and they still keep coming. We are in survival mode right now. All of our operations have been shut down, and we are just trying to keep afloat. The city/government is still not providing electricity or water or even contributing food or fuel. The people can expect absolutely nothing from their elected officials. But in all honesty, how can we expect anything from them when the Presidential Palace has been destroyed along with the departments of Finance, Justice Tax, Education, Foreign Affairs and the Post Office?

Supplies have begun to arrive at the airport this week, but nothing is getting to the people yet. People are living and sleeping in the streets by the thousands trying to find food—looking for anything to eat anywhere they can. Businesses that were left standing cannot open because there is no security. They would be mobbed before they got their doors halfway open. Even should food come into the country via ship, the docks are down, and the one crane that unloads the food supplies is lying at the bottom of the sea.

We made numerous attempts to obtain assistance from many international aid organizations to get food, tents, tarps, etc., but we were turned down. I was surprised that no one would help us—not even some of the Christian aid organizations. I got the impression that the organizations were fighting among themselves while people continued to suffer without food, water, and a place to live. We learned a long time ago that our help does not come from man, but our source is God Himself. You cannot lose with Him by your side.

People are struggling just to stay alive. I see only hopelessness in those sad eyes. The officials are just guessing at the death toll. Some say 100,000, others say 250,000. But the truth is, no one will ever know the true death toll. Complete families have been wiped out, so who can report them missing? Dead bodies are scooped up by machines along with debris and concrete and disposed of without ever being noticed by the machine operators.

January 21, 2010, Thursday
Day 10

We had finally gotten back into our apartment on the third floor. But because of the 6.0 tremor yesterday, we had to leave and return to the volunteer apartment. We thank God for Pastor Stewart Farley from Lewisburg, West Virginia, and Rhema Christian Center, who built these volunteer efficiency apartments for workers who come from the states to help out for short-term projects. We don't know what we would have done without them during this time.

Today, we are beginning to rebuild our wall around our compound. We were blessed to be able to find the cement and block needed for this repair. Even though the cost to purchase these items was astronomically high ($16,000), to have these materials shipped to us in a container would be a far greater expense. This repair is for only a short section of our security wall.

We are working on cleaning out the buildings and salvaging any items that are worth saving. A few streets are open for travel, but many have not been cleared yet. Then, too, some of the open streets have been taken over by people who are using them as temporary homes. We have been able to purchase gas and fuel, but it took $88,000 to do so. As costs mount up, I am so thankful I serve a

God who has a storehouse full of everything we need and workers willing to bring that storehouse to us.

January 29, 2010, Friday
Day 18

Today, we received a truckload of food from *World Food*. We also received a shipment of food purchased by a church in Huntington, West Virginia, that was brought via the Dominican Republic border. We have distributed to the people everything we have been able to. There are 40,000 lbs. of rice given to us by *Feed My Starving Children* in December, 2009, that was still at the port waiting to be unloaded when the earthquake hit. We are trying to find out the status of this food from the military and Haitians working at the port. No one seems to know anything about this food.

February 1, 2010, Monday
Day 21

Haiti is truly a land of tears—tears being shed by people who have lost loved ones and tears shed from those who have lost all their worldly possessions. There are tears of fear of what is going to happen in the times ahead. But then, there are tears of joy, too—joy when you find the loved one alive that you have been searching for since the earthquake happened and tears of joy as an offering of thanks to God for His provisions.

Although we have not been able to get reports from all our locations or visit them ourselves, we know we have lost many, many lives and hundreds from our congregations are in the hospitals throughout the country. Some of our injured have been taken to the north to Cap-Haïtien to get help at hospitals there. From the reports, we have learned that at least 6 of our 42 churches and/or schools have major damages or will need to be replaced. At this time, we are still waiting on reports from the others.

February 6, 2010, Saturday
Day 26

I have spent the last week visiting our churches and schools to assess the damages. We have lost staff members, church members, and children, and our hearts are heavy with these family losses. We have many that are in hospitals and some that are now amputees. At the time of the earthquake, IMO had over 218 workers on our payrolls. This included pastors, teachers, directors, school cooks, nurses, and maintenance personnel. These people are the core of IMO, and without them, we cannot possibly do all that we do. These are faces we know and love and work with every day. They aren't just statistics. Just about all of them lost their home and everything they had. Our workers and congregations are without homes, and the rainy season is on its way. Dear Lord, help me to help them!

We have established a temporary shelter in Boutin, about 35 miles from our headquarters in Delmas. There, we have several school buildings and a church that are being used as housing facilities. We estimate we can take in around 2,000 people even though a portion of the church is missing. The medical clinic has some repairable damage and can be used to treat the injured and sick. We have a well, a kitchen, a dining hall, a school, and housing for disabled people there already. We have purchased 15 vinyl tents, and when these tents arrive, they will provide temporary shelter from the sun and rain. Fifteen is a good start, but we need many more to house all the homeless people.

February 8, 2010, Monday
Day 28

We have finally been able to get back into our apartment where we live. So many things were broken and destroyed, but do not misunderstand me, I am not complaining. We are glad just to be alive.

It has been four weeks since the first 7.0 earthquake hit, and we know Haiti is fading out of the world news limelight. Since January 12, reporters have been roaming around seeking out the most sensational stories to pass on to their viewers, but now they are all beginning to return back to their homes, moving on to the next big world event. *We* do not get to move on. Millions are still without food and shelter. Many have never seen the first bag of relief efforts. Large organizations have food but do not possess the ability on the local level to get it distributed. IMO and other long-term organizations in Haiti have the ability to distribute large quantities of food to thousands of people, but the large organizations will not give us any supplies. These large organizations have their own agenda, and we small outreaches are not on that agenda! Shipping lines are dictated to supply the large organizations first, but the large organizations do not have the connections to the locals to get the job done. What a cycle of frustration!

When we bring supplies via the Dominican Republic border, our order of supplies arrives considerably lighter than when it started. Thieves wanting to make a quick profit help themselves to our supplies before they even get close to our warehouse. Even in the best of times, getting supplies shipped in is a big headache. But now, all the headaches are compounded and multiplied.

In coordination with our daughter, Faithe Claxton, our Director of Operations in the States, construction supplies, tents, generators, household items, and food are beginning to arrive at our warehouse in Clendenin, West Virginia. Our long-time supporters and contributors are joining us in making this effort come together. Tools and generators have been donated by the folks in Fayetteville, North Carolina, and supplies are being dropped off at local businesses and schools in the Clendenin area and brought to our warehouse. Our daughter, Cindy, has started a food and money drive at her beauty salon in Virginia, and many donations have already come in. A 90-year-old soldier of the Lord from Detroit, Michigan, Hulda Huff, has pledged to make 100 quilts and blankets and is halfway there. Various construction companies throughout the United States who have been our loyal supporters for years are joining together to get the construction material and equipment we desperately need to do repairs on our schools and churches.

For now, the schools are shut down. Although the Haitian government wants all schools not affected by the earthquake damages to remain open, we will keep ours closed until the unstable aftershocks have ceased. We feel it is best to keep all children away from any potential falling buildings due to the continuing aftershocks. The loss of one child would be one child too many.

We are continuing to feed the children every day at our school locations, since most of them have food that was distributed prior to the earthquake. During this time, we are continuing to pay our teachers and directors, so we hope the support for the children's sponsorship program will continue to come in.

February 12, 2010, Friday
Day 32

What a great day today has been for the people of Haiti! At 6:00 a.m. people began congregating in our Delmas church here on the compound. President Rene Preval has cancelled Mardi Gras and declared a three-day period of fasting and prayer for the country of Haiti. I never thought I would live to see Mardi Gras cancelled! Normally, Mardi Gras here in Haiti is a time for a lot of people to party all night long and forget their responsibilities. It is a time when crime and drunkenness reaches an all-time high. The motto is "pleasure only" and "forget" the consequences. Due to a large amount of vandalism and violence, Mardi Gras is not our favorite time of the year. But what a difference it is this year!

To start the three-day fast, over 4,000 people attended our services here on the Delmas compound. A tarp for shelter was hung over the schoolyard to cover the people standing outside listening to the service going on inside. The paved entrance to the front of the church was lined with people—even out into the streets on both sides—singing and clapping their hands, praising God for His mercy and grace. It was like this all over the country in all the churches. And if there wasn't a church available for people to attend, streets were blocked off, and thousands gathered from 6:00 a.m. to 12:00 noon for services to praise our Lord and Savior.

We had some reports from four of our churches that said there were over 500 people who gave their hearts to Christ! What is it that 2 Chronicles says? "If my people who are called by my name, will humble themselves and pray and seek my face, and turn from their wicked ways: then I will hear from heaven, and I will forgive their sin and will heal their land" (NIV). Oh, for America to take notice and humble herself before God and for the people to begin praying for God to heal our land!

We are still delivering food as it comes in to us and are trying to purchase more tents and tarps for our people as the rains have started now. Yesterday, Joyce went to the medical clinic in Boutin and ran into a downpour. She and her nurses saw over 120 patients, and she reported that there are already many children running high fevers. Dr. Ken, from Texas, is coming next week to go with Joyce and the nurses to Boutin where he will help doctor the sick in the homeless families we have taken in.

As always, when Joyce travels out to the remote areas in the country, she takes a sandwich and drink for lunch. There are no Burger Kings or KFCs along the way or out in the brush areas to stop for a quick lunch. There aren't even any convenience stores to hop in for a coke and a sweet roll. Just heat, dirt, and dust. But today, she gave her sandwich and drink to one little girl who was hungry. She said it was worth it when the little girl, before she left, turned and smiled at her thanking her graciously for the wonderful gifts. That, my friend, is what serving Jesus is all about! Jesus said, "If you have done unto the least of these, you have done it unto me." When we help one small child who is hungry, hurting or suffering, it is worth all the effort and money it takes to provide that help. It is also worth the sacrifices we make in not being able to be with our own children and grandchildren on special occasions and at family gatherings. It is a calling that comes from God, and only He knows why He has called us to make these sacrifices.

February 13, 2010, Saturday
Day 33

We have two containers at our warehouse in Clendenin that are being loaded with supplies this week brought in from our supporters in North Carolina, Virginia, Ohio, Missouri, Arkansas, Tennessee, Washington, D.C., and many more states. If all goes well, these containers should arrive here in Haiti in approximately ten days. We are scheduling work groups in the near future to come in from the States to help us rebuild and repair, and we hope to reopen our Bible school the first of March. We are starting to move forward, and we realize it is going to take a lot of people "staying the course" to get these monumental tasks completed. But one thing I pray, Dear God, is for us not to lose our main focus for being here: souls—the salvation of one soul from hell will make it seem as nothing when we stand before our Master.

February 19, 2010, Friday
Day 39

Dr. Ken arrived and went with Joyce to Boutin to the medical clinic today. It was a long day for him as he saw over 200 children who were suffering from malnutrition and various other illnesses associated with the earthquake and poverty. Thank God for our supporters who are helping us minister to these children and are saving lives.

Pastor Clint Block and his church, Calvary Full Gospel in Forsyth, Missouri, have sent us vinyl cloths to make tents. Someone in his church contacted some billboard companies and got them to donate over 100 vinyl cloths that are used for making billboard signs. Pastor Clint came to Haiti to show us how to make a wonderful tent by taking one inch PVC pipes and attaching them with fittings. IMO will never forget this great effort of love. [Many of these people have lived for over two years under these tents.]

Dear God, the needs keep mounting up, and I have to keep reminding myself the real reason for being here is to preach Your Word. We are here to preach Your Word and Your plan of salvation. And we must let You, God, supply the needs. You know these people are hurting and have lost family, homes, and possessions, and we pray that we can, through You, give them encouragement and help them find hope for the future. Our big commission here in Haiti has gotten so much bigger, but we know we can do it with Your help because You tell us in Your Word that NOTHING IS IMPOSSIBLE WITH YOU! **Amen.**

A common Port-au-Prince scene after the earthquake of 2010.
Most homes have never been replaced or repaired.

CHAPTER 23

Journal of A Mission Trip To Haiti

Let us not grow weary in doing good, for at the proper time we will reap a harvest if we do not give up. Galatians 6:9 (NIV)

AS I HAVE stressed before, it is so very important to know where your donations are going. That is why we invite and encourage everyone to take a trip across the North Atlantic Ocean to our headquarters in Haiti.

In October 2010, Pastor Wesley Pritchard, senior pastor from the Fayetteville Community Church in Fayetteville, North Carolina, made his first trip to IMO Headquarters. Pastor Pritchard's father and previous pastor of Fayetteville Community Church, Ken W. Pritchard, 76, also went along on the trip. Ken has been a long-time supporter of IMO and a visitor to Haiti over ten times with groups from his church. The following journal is a day-to-day account of what Pastor Wesley Pritchard and the ten men who went with him experienced on their trip to Haiti.

Monday, October 4, 2010
3:00 a.m.

When my alarm went off this morning, I awoke in my nice warm bed in Fayetteville, North Carolina. I went over my packing check list: candy for the children, lightweight clothes to wear in the hot climate, my digital camera, my video camera and of course, my beloved iPad. Oh yes, and all my hair care products. What would all the guys tease me about if I didn't wear my salt and pepper hair spiked and full of styling gel!

I thought my packing was complete. What I didn't realize at the time, I had not packed any equipment to prepare my heart for the things I was about to experience nor glasses for the things my eyes were about to see!

4:00 a.m.

The Missions Team met in the parking lot of Fayetteville Community Church, packed and ready to leave for the airport. From our church there was Buster Livengood and Daniel Bain, both electricians going on their fourth trip; Ronnie Goodman, welder, first trip; Rick Salyer, recording engineer, first trip; Earl Griffen, handyman, first trip; Jimmy Hobbs, building contractor, first trip; Herb Parsons, retired US Army who works fulltime at our church in charge of all buildings, ten plus trips; and Greg Renfrow, who works for US Foods, and this was his first trip. From Stone Harbor Church in Fayetteville, there was Pastor Bill and George, and this was their first trip also.

I was pretty much going on a sightseeing trip with a little bit of videotaping on the side, but the other guys had lots of work to do, like repair roofs damaged in the recent tornado and installing an electric gate closer. The guest bathrooms at the headquarters also had to be remodeled due to earthquake damage.

Dad, Pastor John, and several of the Haitian pastors who have visited our church have been after me for years to go to Haiti. I think I knew deep down it was going to impact me so as to change my life, and I wasn't sure I wanted my life to change.

We had prayer, and then we were all ready to leave the familiar, the comfort, and security of what we called home. I didn't know I was on my way to one of the most uncomfortable places on the face of this earth.

The flight from North Carolina to Florida was uneventful, as well as the flight from Florida to Haiti. We had the normal wait and hurry up or hurry up and wait scenarios, but those delays just gave the team a chance to get closer acquainted and do a little bit of male bonding. The camaraderie was great amid the laughter and stories told on one another. Upon arrival in Port-au-Prince, the uneventful changed so quickly to more activity happening to us than our five senses could ever begin to absorb!

Go this way! Go that way! With Pastor John at the helm, we were pulled and pushed through the small, crowded airport from the time we landed on Haitian soil until we exited customs and immigration. It was so hot and sticky, kinda reminded me of a hot August afternoon in the south, only the smells were much worse. When we cleared customs we claimed our luggage, well most of it. Mr. Earl couldn't find his suitcase, and he was about one toothbrush away from shedding tears. We left the airport with 18 pieces of bags, one short of what we had when we started the trip.

Wow! The pushing and shoving continued outside in the crowds surrounding the airport. You really don't know whom to trust at all. You feel vulnerable at every turn. The Haitian men stand around like bell caps trying to grab your bags acting like they want to help you, but what they want is for you to feel obligated to give them money for their service. Even if they touch your bag—and I mean *touch* your bag, they expect you to give them money. And if you don't, they appear insulted. It's a little scary. The only thing I can say is having Pastor John with us was the only reason why we came out of the airport safely! We finally made our way to the Chevy Suburban and the red Ford dump truck that were waiting to transport us to our destination. Herb, Buster, Pastor Bill, Earl, and I joined Pastor John in the suburban. I look up, and there is my 76-year-old Dad crawling into the back of the dump truck that has all our luggage. The dump truck only had rails on the sides, and the back was open. Joining Dad in the back of the dump truck were Greg, Daniel, George, Ronnie, Rick, and riding shotgun was Jimmy. Jimmy told me later that as soon as he got in the cab of the dump truck, Maxo, his driver, told him to lock his door. I guess that was one memo that didn't reach the guys that were in the back of the dump truck!

More pushing and shoving, except now it was with our vehicles. Pastor John, "Pas" as the Haitians call him, says, "You can't give any of the other drivers eye contact, because if you do, they got you! You just have to push your way on through." Hmmmm . . . comforting, especially for our dump truck buddies. I pulled out my video camera and tried to video the trip from the airport. Wow, what bumps and potholes! We were being tossed and shaken from side to side like a "Tilt a Wheel" at a carnival. I kept trying to watch out for my daddy in the dump truck but to no avail. I had to believe that someone much greater than me had His hand on him and his dump truck buddies. Why Daddy got in that dump truck I still don't know. The last thing Mom told me was "not to let your daddy be breathing in all that dust over there, and remember, he has a pacemaker!"

I was constantly looking back and forth, side to side, filth, destruction—doesn't seem strong enough words to describe the poverty . . . again not strong enough . . . helplessness, maybe hopelessness—I am seeing. In need of a Savior . . . yes, that's it. Tent city after tent city, blocks of rubble, buildings in ruin, lives ruined, cars blowing horn after horn, my head spinning trying to take it all in but, at the same time, wishing I could forget it too. Bumping and pulling going on in the truck, all the time "Pas" laughing and telling his stories. I told him, "Pastor John, I have never loved you so much as right now."

I look at Pastor John and Maxo, our lives in their hands, dust flying off the roads, children trying to play with busted basketballs right in front of our trucks . . . more tent cities . . . more people . . . more filth . . . more bumping and pulling . . . more trying to find my dad . . . people walking way too close to our trucks, more destruction, more rubble. I guess the rubble on the ground can't compare to the rubble of the lives that are here.

Finally, we arrived at the IMO compound in Delmas, and the massive steel gate opened and then closed behind us. I have never been so glad that someone told me I had to be behind bars! The compound is very nice in every way. It really is a safe haven, if there *is* a place in Haiti to feel safe. Pastor John showed us around the compound telling us every detail about the warehouse, the generator room, the guest quarters, the living quarters, the observation deck . . . all I could do was cry. I looked at a few of our team . . . Rick Salyer was speechless, Greg Renfrow was crying too, Ronnie Goodman was beaming, because he just found the welder he will use for building the new gate closers for the compound. Did I mention Ronnie loves to weld? Daniel Bain, Jimmy Hobbs, and Buster Livengood were busy assessing the tasks at hand. Earl Griffen was wondering will he ever have a clean shirt, and will he have to wear Jimmy's underwear the whole week? Herb Parsons was "herbing," a new phrase the group coined for Herb doing what he does best—being "large and in charge!" (Pastor Ken, my dad, was watching us all to see our responses. He wanted to make sure we all don't miss seeing the vision of what we need to do in Haiti.)

6:00 p.m.

Dinner was amazing! Country cooking comes to Haiti. All of the Haitian women folks were serving US style. We felt like we should have been serving them. Pastor John and Ms. Joyce began telling us stories about the terrible days following the earthquake and God's goodness, and His protection, and His sustaining power over them. Their stories were sad but amazing too.

9:00 p.m.

After a snack of popcorn, Dad and I went to our room over in the apartment guesthouse, and all the other guys bunked in the two guest rooms off the main kitchen and living area of the guest house. I hope there's no fighting on who gets the top or bottom bunk beds!

Tuesday, October 5, 2010
8:00 a.m.

A breakfast of eggs, bacon, biscuits, and gravy was served. Really makes me miss my pop-tarts at home. We all listened to Pastor John tell us what he wanted us to do today. Jimmy, Earl, Greg, and George are to begin remodeling the guest bathrooms with new cabinets and toilets. They have a real incentive to get them done today because they are the bathrooms they will be using!

Buster and Daniel are to begin running wire for the new gate closers. Dad, myself, Pastor Bill, Rick, and Ronnie will go with Pastor John to Bon Repos (meaning a "place of peace") to measure some things Ronnie and Rick are going to build. As we head out to Bon Repos, we see more poverty stricken areas and earthquake devastation, more tent cities—thousands upon thousands of displaced people.

On the way back from Bon Repos, we see a dead body in the road covered by a sheet. Someone had been hit by a car, and all the people were standing around waiting for the dead man's family to come and claim the body and for the police to come. We all kinda freaked out. Pastor John said "It's just another day in Haiti, someone dying in the streets." He then tells us more about the days following the earthquake and the over 300,000 dead and dying in the streets and the massive graves outside the city. I don't want to write any more about that.

10:30 a.m.

Lots of work is going on back in the compound. Jimmy is sweating up a storm. Buster is red-faced, Ronnie is thrilled that he is about to weld something . . . anything. Work goes on throughout day two.

1:00 p.m.

Burgers and fries, and this amazing hot cabbage dish called "pickling" was served for lunch. That "pickling" makes anything taste great. The school kids are out in the playground next door, and Greg went and got a soccer ball, a Frisbee, and a football. We gave them to the kids, and it was like Christmas! More tears. You wish you had something to give to every one of the kids. It is so hard to know who to give the gifts to. We gave candy to the teacher to pass out. Whew, that was a good move. If you have ever fed the "carp" at the beach, you have an idea of what it felt like. Survival of the fittest. Every hand wanting a piece of something, anything. Nothing was left behind, not even one small piece of candy; even the pieces that fell to the ground were scarfed up quickly.

I had a couple pairs of sunglasses. I gave one to a little girl who just kept hugging me and had the most adorable smile. Then I noticed a little boy sitting alone on the benches. He hadn't been playing with the other children and again my heart pounds. Why does he sit alone? I went over and sat beside him and gave him the other pair of sunglasses. He beamed a bright smile to me. Before I could enjoy that big smile, a large boy came along and took them away from him. Well, let me tell you, the grandpa in me came alive, and I went over to that big boy and told him in my best North Carolina redneck language to give those sunglasses back to my new friend. Now, I know he couldn't understand exactly what I was saying, but he got my message loudly and clearly. He took the sunglasses back to the little boy, and, once again, I saw the smile that had wooed me over. "Merci, merci," my new friend said to me as he hugged me once again. More tears. I walked back to help the guys working on the door closer and remembered what Ms. Joyce said about having only 1,600 sponsors for the 5,000 students in their schools. I wonder, what are we doing? And why?

6:00 p.m.

The sun is setting on another day in Haiti, and the team is tired. One gate closer is completed. The security gate for Bon Repos, that Ronnie was measuring for this morning, is almost complete. He and Rick said they had to work on it in their "spare time" from helping Daniel and Buster with the gate closer. The bathroom project turned out to be more work than expected. You just can't run down to Lowes and get what you need, so you have to improvise a lot. Jimmy and the crew have been up and down the second floor steps to the guest house at least 150 times or more today, says Jimmy. It was stifling hot up there in the bathrooms, and I really feel sorry for those boys.

7:00 p.m.

We all met for dinner, and it was unbelievable. Fried chicken, green beans, fried plantain, and again my favorite—pickling. The conversation around the table tonight was mainly with Ms. Joyce. Did I mention how much I love her? Her sweet spirit is amazing, and the tone of her voice could set a grizzly bear at ease. She spoke of when she was here during the years of rioting and street gangs. She compared it to "Black Hawk Down" and the fighting in Mogadishu. Having seen that movie scares me for her and Pastor John. She also talked about the earthquake and how that 37 percent of the total people who were killed were students and teachers. That is 37 percent of 300,000 were students and teachers. Mind boggling. She cried as she began telling us about one of the Haitian pastors whose daughter died at the university and how they could hear her voice from beneath the building rubble that had fallen on her. They could hear her, but no one could get her out in time to save her life.

Pastor John came in late and was his usual jovial self. He's a mixture of Santa Claus, Billy Graham, Larry the Cable Guy, and Steven Segal all rolled up into one amazing individual—happy, compassionate, funny, and strong. He is always saying "Amen" and not scared of anything—except not being able to help the next child in need that comes through the compound gate.

10:00 p.m.

Dad and I walked through lighting and pouring rain back to our room, and I begin journaling my day. Buster has been asleep for a couple of hours. Jimmy, instead of counting sheep, is still recounting the number of times he went up and down the stairs. Greg tells us all how much he misses his wife and how he has never been away from her this long. Earl's suitcase is still not here, maybe tomorrow. Thankfully, he has loaner underwear, pants, and clean shirts. Daniel is washing his other clothes for tomorrow. Rick is wondering what welding project will thrill Ronnie in the morning to come. A hot shower will feel so good to wash the Haitian dirt and grime off of all of us. There isn't anything strong enough to wash away the memories of the day. They are etched in our minds and hearts forever.

Wednesday, October 6, 2010
9:00 a.m.

After a great hot breakfast of pancakes, bacon, and eggs, we head out to Petigot. The journey to Petigot seemed forever. IMO has a church and a school at Petigot, and it happens to be where the two children live that my wife, Teresa, and I sponsor. On our way to Petigot, the road was blocked because they were installing interlocking pavers in a little village. Ms. Joyce and the guys with her paid some locals to move the blocks so we could pass. Pastor John, who didn't want to wait for the blocks to be moved, took, well, let's just call it "the more scenic route" around and around and around until we finally made it back to the main road. Wow, it's really hard to call any road here a *main* road.

When we got to Petigot, I found out the little girl that we sponsor had typhoid and was at the hospital, but I did meet Louissart, the very shy 15-year-old boy we sponsor who says he wants to be a chauffeur when he grows up. A chauffeur in Haiti is a driver of a "Tap-Tap," a pickup truck painted to the max with colorful paint and sayings written all over them. Most of them look as though they could break down at any moment. Every Tap-Tap is crowded with people hanging on to every inch possible, trying to get to where they need to be.

On the way back, the locals who we paid to move the blocks, had stacked the stones back in the road. Except this time, they had used larger boulders. My guess was they were "upping the ante." Some of our guys got out and moved the stones out of the way. It was much more economical, but Pastor John said it was "much more dangerous." The locals didn't like it at all, us taking their "highway tax money" away, and Pastor said they could begin throwing those rocks at us any moment. It is funny that rock throwers like Ernest T. Bass are also in Haiti!

1:30 p.m.

Back at the compound, thankfully! Earl's suitcase hasn't showed up yet. The whole team just looks whipped. We really didn't do any work on the trip; all we did was drive out there and back, but the four-hour trip was terribly hard on all of us. We felt like we had been put in a blender and left on high for four hours. I don't see how John and Joyce do it day after day after day. God's grace and protection must always be on them. Especially for their health. The constant beating on your body is brutal. I have just three more days till I am driving again at home on the Eisenhower Interstate System. There isn't one road that we have been on that compares to any roads back in the States. Even the worse pothole-filled roads in the northeast are so much better than the roads here. Dad said the road into Greasy Creek, where he is from in western North Carolina, is so much better.

We all had lunch together, and then everyone split to get started back on his project. Daniel and Ronnie began another project from their list of projects. Dad and I went to our room. I am speaking and singing tonight in a church service at Terre Rouge. I confess, I am very scared. I have never spoken through a translator before. I pray that if Edner, my translator, doesn't know what I am talking about, the Lord will give him another message that he and the people will understand. Lord, help me!

4:30 p.m.

We walk out of our room into the 109 degree afternoon and see something we have been waiting for all week. Earl is beaming! They found his luggage, and it is finally on the way to the compound. His bag had been mistakenly taken by a Lutheran man named Currin, who was on a mission trip to Haiti too. We found out that he was doing his mission work at a four-star resort along the north coast called Wahoo Bay Resort. I didn't know such a place existed in Haiti. Thankfully, he finally saw it in his heart to return the luggage filled with Earl's heart medication. Well, those pills were actually "Skittles," but Earl did say they were good for his heart.

We took off shortly for the church service at Terre Rouge, and once again got to experience the streets filled with potholes and washed out ruts. After an endless drive, we finally reached an area with a beautiful mountain range in front of us. Greg said that if he had to live in a tent and be homeless in Haiti, this was where he wanted to be. It reminded all of us of the California mountains where there is nothing but flat, flat, flat lands and then all of a sudden you're climbing up the steep, steep mountains.

While driving and climbing up these steep mountain roads, you begin dodging cattle, burrows, horses, donkeys, and ugly, ugly dogs. And I can't forget the Haitian filet mignon: goat. The climb to the church was so steep and treacherous that Dad kept telling Pastor John to stay away from the edge. Dad is really one to be telling someone how to drive in the mountains. I have ridden with him through the mountains of North Carolina and have had my own white knuckles and eyes wide shut.

6:30 p.m.

We arrive at the Terre Rouge church that sits even up higher on a hill. There are no cars in the parking lot, because no one owns a car in this remote area. People walked for miles and miles in the dark from all over the mountain to get to this newly constructed church. Pastor John told us he had almost lost a perfectly good bulldozer and a dozer operator over the side of the cliff when he was building the church. That information is really comforting when you are standing on the church porch that has no railings and looking over the edge that has a drop so steep from which no man could ever return!

The people were slow to gather, but when they were all there, the praise and worship hits full force with a marching bass drum and my personal favorites: tambourines, a guy playing what looks to be two pieces of one-half inch plate steel he constructed with a handle that he bangs together on the upbeat, and another homemade instrument that has long, round steel sides with small nail holes punched in it. The musician uses a piece of metal to slide it up and down on beats two and four. "Wichita" is playing a guitar. Rick and I gave him the name "Wichita" after our favorite guitar man, and two girls are singing through the same ten-inch guitar amp that the guitar and Casio keyboard are plugged into. Thank goodness no one played the keyboard! You can't imagine how loud it was in that small church. The metal roof and concrete walls reverberated sound throughout the whole quiet mountain valley.

Then the people started singing, and the decibel level raised another 50 percent at least. About now in some of our churches at home they would be complaining that it was too loud and needed to be turned down. But you couldn't turn these people down if you tried! It would have been impossible to turn down the volume of their joy and sincerity or the smiling and sheer jubilance and elation of the emotion that was emanating in that church. I leaned over to Rick and said, "Can you believe their amazing overflowing joy—and yet they have nothing!" In our country, we have everything, and people still have the need to fill their bodies with anti-depressants and every other kind of medicine available. Hmmm . . . makes you think what is truly important in life to have. Jesus . . . the Joy of the Lord is my strength says the Word of God—not the joy of my possessions.

One of the sweetest things that happened tonight was the story the founding pastor of the church told as he stood in front of the congregation. The pastor walks to church every service, which in itself is a miracle since he is 95 years old. The average life expectancy here for males is late 50s. The pastor recounted the history of the church and how long it had been a brush arbor church without a real permanent building. He told the people that he had prayed to God and asked him that before he died, he would give him a permanent building where the people of the village could marry, have funerals, and where people could be saved, healed, and filled with the Holy Spirit. He looked around at all the people gathered in the church and cried. "This is my dream come true," he said, with tears streaming down his face. Wow, more tears from all of us.

We were getting ready to go, when Greg and I found some candy in the back of the truck left from our day in Petigot. So, we began passing it out to the children. I quickly felt the mob of kids pushing in. I gave the bag to Greg and ran for cover back in the church. That is when I saw Pastor John. He was sitting at a dinner table prepared for us. Now, up to this time, we had been given instructions to not drink the water or eat the food unless it was OKed by them. And here is John motioning for us to come over to the table and telling us it will be OK. Edner prayed for the food, and somewhere in his prayer, I think he prayed the words in the Bible that say "if you eat any deadly thing it will not harm you." We all stood on that Bible verse and had our first experience with goat. Actually Rick and Greg had two helpings, and they said it wasn't "baaaad" at all.

Pastor Edner made my first preaching experience with a translator easy. All went well, and after the sermon, the altar was filled with people for us to lay hands on and pray for. I think many lives were changed because we made that trip to the little mountain church. I know all the lives from North Carolina were changed that night by experiencing the unspeakable joy of the little church on the top of the mountain at Terre Rouge.

Returning back to the compound, we dodged more animals, barely missed the broken stalled out truck with no lights, dodged the people walking along the side of the road . . . no, in the road. Then just for additional fun, it rained, and we got to drive through water gushing down every street. The water washed all the trash and debris down the hills that had accumulated in the tent cities filling the streets with everything imaginable. Pastor John's main concern was *what* we were running over in the streets that we couldn't see. After a few more rain-filled craters, we arrived back at the compound. Ms. Joyce and her helpers had a small snack of Haitian grits, rice, beef shank, cabbage, and pickling, ready for those of us who hadn't eaten heartily of the meal at Terre Rouge. After the snack, we all departed to get ready for day four.

Thursday, October 7, 2010
7:30 a.m.

This morning, we walked out of our apartment into the worst humidity I have ever felt. With no air movement, the atmosphere was thick and muggy with a slight drizzle of rain. We all agreed it was about as bad as we had ever felt. The mood at the breakfast table was jovial as everyone was teasing Earl about setting his alarm clock every two or three hours during the night just to change into his clean clothes. They said he was trying to catch up for three days of the same shirt and shorts.

Greg has a new name; they're calling him Billy because he ate so much goat last night at Terre Rouge. The guys accused him of sounding like the old Saturday Night Live character "goat boy" who says every word with a "naaaa" sound.

9:00 a.m.

Ms. Joyce asked us to get candy and stuff to give to the kids at the Delmas School. Enrollment at Delmas School is around 370, and it can change from day to day. Jimmy Hobbs got to meet one of the kids he and his wife, Leslie, sponsor. The little girl, who was 13 years old, and her dad had walked four miles, rode a Tap-Tap 13 miles, and had made the five-hour hour journey to meet Jimmy, her sponsor, at 9:00 this morning. Jimmy was flabbergasted. "They did all that just for a 15-dollar backpack, some candy, a few items, and a picture with me!"

We were met by a kind and gracious principal, at the Delmas School located on the compound. He was a very sharp Haitian man who had a seminary degree and a Master's in education. He and Ms. Joyce took us from classroom to classroom where we visited kindergarten grades up through sixth grade. Clean, very clean, well-behaved children were in every classroom. We gave them beanie babies, candy, and left over "united" lights. The lights were a definite hit. I wish we had had thousands of those flash lights to pass out. In the tents where these kids live, there are no lights, and I would say maybe one candle for every tent that I have seen. You just never see any light. So giving these kids a small flashlight was huge!

11:00 a.m.

All kinds of work is going on and around the compound. Ronnie and Rick are still welding doorframes for the new compound at Bon Repos. Ronnie's back is hurting him pretty bad, and the guys have all laid hands on him and prayed for him after breakfast. Buster and Daniel are working on moving an old generator out and putting a new one in. A huge undertaking that is! Dad is resting for a minute. The humidity drains him so fast. Herb is "herbing" somewhere. The other guys are helping Jimmy with cabinet installation in the bathrooms and various other building and repair projects on the compound. Although the earthquake didn't demolish the buildings on the compound, a lot of minor damage was done and needs to be repaired.

1:00 p.m.

Daniel still isn't back with Panyel from the electric supply store. He is trying to get parts so the old generator can be moved and a new one put in. Buster doesn't think they will be able to find what they need to complete the job. Everything is so difficult here.

Pastor John, Jimmy, and I have left the compound for an all-day excursion to Bois Léger, Drouillard, and Boutin. Again, I know this seems like a stuck record, but it takes us forever to get to these three places. We drove in a four-wheel drive for miles and miles of endless mud holes. Bois Léger and Drouillard both had sustained structural damage to their roofs during a recent violent wind storm. Both are in need of major repair. In Bois Léger, the roof actually flew off one of their buildings onto some folks' house and damaged their roof. So Jimmy measured the items we would need to fix it tomorrow. While we were there, one of the ladies asked us to go and pray for the founding pastor's wife. She was lying down inside a small hut, and it was so hot in there that even a healthy person would have had trouble breathing. I watched as Pastor John leaned in to listen intently to what she said. The sweat was pouring off of him, and his shirt was so wet, it looked as if he had been in one of the many mud holes we drove through. We all laid hands on her and prayed for her healing. Another day in Haiti . . . More tears.

After Bois Léger, we went on to Boutin. My Dad had been telling me for years he wanted me to see Boutin. Some years back, our church had sent a construction team to erect a roof on the round church there. I had heard that it was so desolate and dry. A real desert of a place. What we saw today was one of the nicest greenest places we have seen since being in Haiti. This is the rainy season, so everything there was nice and green. The houses were all kept nice, and there is a new church and a clinic for medical teams to come and offer medical assistance to the folks of that region. We measured some newly constructed houses there for the possibility to return and construct more houses, a kitchen, and a dining house. I was told that this was the first place where John and Joyce had begun their ministry, and from what I saw, God was definitely blessing the first fruits of their works.

5:00 p.m.

We get back in the Chevy pickup with mud dripping from everywhere all over it. I told Pastor John that, in the morning, somebody will have a big job cleaning up this one. Pastor John explained to me that every morning at the compound the vehicles are washed and fueled up for the next day's journeys. IMO has the cleanest and most reliable vehicles I have seen in all of Haiti. I really thank the Lord for that.

As we head through the bog out of Boutin, I am thinking, "Hallelujah, we are heading back to the compound." But, nooooo, we aren't heading that way at all. We haven't been to Drouillard yet, and Pastor John splashes through a huge ditch and heads that way to see another church whose roof has blown off. Now, I am thinking, "OK Pastor John, you have got me, I am on board wholeheartedly with you. You don't really have to show me something else that needs to be done here."

Then I remembered what Ms. Joyce had told me earlier today. We had been passing out sunglasses to some of the school kids. I had already given some out and had, maybe, 16 pairs left. There weren't enough for everyone in the class. I looked at her and said, "I wish there was enough, enough for everybody." She looked at me with huge tears and said, "Is there ever enough?" More tears and more of the reality of what real "need" is here. I am crying while typing this.

We're on the road again heading back to the compound, and the roads are filled with cars and people heading who knows where. Pastor John tells us how he was called to Haiti and how Ms. Joyce cried when he told her that God had called him here. He said she wasn't crying because she didn't want to come. She was crying because God had told her the same thing! Then they sold everything and moved here. You can't come to a place like this unless God calls you. You would never survive. You would always be looking over your shoulder and wondering "what if?"

8:00 p.m.

I have never cried watching an electric gate open. But tonight I did, because I was so glad to be out of that truck. Our pants were filthy from getting in and out and rubbing them on the mud covered running boards. The guesthouse at the compound was a welcome site. I jumped out and started screaming, "Soccer balls, soccer balls." Someone had purchased a big trash can full of soccer balls. I had told the boys at the Delmas school that I would try to bring them a soccer ball, and now I could keep my promise. Whew, thank you, Jesus. Inside, everyone had eaten and was sitting around listening to our stories as we ate our supper. Jimmy went over what tools and supplies we were going to need for the next morning's list of chores. I could tell everyone was dogged tired. Dad admonished us all not to "get weary in well doing" Galatians 6:9. It was a perfect verse to end the day.

10:30 p.m.

I've just had a shower, and I am feeling human again. Dad and I talked over the events of the day, and now he is asleep. I am so thankful that I got to be here in Haiti with him, and I am really thankful that God has instilled in him the desire to help Pastor John and Joyce, and Dad is passing the vision on to me. I am so thankful to be here in Haiti seeing it all for myself. The harvest is plentiful, but the laborers are few. Not everyone can weld like Ronnie or wire like Buster or Daniel or cheer folks on like my dad can, but everyone can do their part. Ephesians 4:16 says we are all fitted together and each one has their own part. I want more than ever to do mine . . . .

Friday, October 8, 2010
7:30 a.m.

Dad and I head for breakfast and find that all the other guys are there already. I guess none of them have to use as many hair products as Dad and I do. I asked Ms. Joyce's advice on how to distribute the ten soccer balls to the school boys. There really isn't a fair way, she says. We tried to give the sunglasses out based on their grades. You know little Haitian kids will tell you a fib to get a pair of sunglasses. What would they tell you for a soccer ball? The soccer ball is the most prized piece of sporting equipment in Haiti. I think they really need ESPN to get MLB and the NFL here to make some sports equipment donations.

9:00 a.m.

Chapel is in full force, and we can hear the kids singing. Beautiful sounds. Ms. Joyce says now is the time to go over there. We found seven boys in the school yard and no one else. By now they recognize me and the guys. Pastor John tells them to line up. They get in a straight line, and I begin to distribute the balls. Man, does Santa Claus have a cool job or what! I have never felt any better about anything I have ever done than being able to keep my word to those boys and coming through with these soccer balls. All the commotion made by the new soccer balls was heard in the school, and pretty soon the yard was full of kids. That same question, "is there ever enough," was forming in my mind. The little man that stole my heart earlier in the week came down in the first group, and I am so glad that he was one of the boys who got the last three soccer balls. I taught him and some of the boys to give me a high five sign and say "My man." I don't ever think I will hear those words and not remember my kids at Delmas School.

9:30 a.m.

We are headed to Bois Léger. All the tools are loaded in the dump truck, and the rest of us pile in two other trucks. At the last minute, Dad decided to stay back. It is so hot for him, and I know it saps his strength. Ronnie and Pastor Bill stay back to try to finish the welding projects. We drive on through the same horrible streets, and the sun is so hot. So much for getting an early start before the noon heat!

11:30 a.m.

We arrived at Bois Léger, and let me just say it is so strange here in Haiti when you arrive at a place. At first you don't see anyone at all, and then maybe one or two people show up, and before you know it, there are people everywhere watching and talking up a storm. They will also laugh at you. It makes you want to be able to communicate with them, but all you can do is just smile at them and wait for that large smile coming back at you.

Pastor John and I are working on a promo video that is a short one- to two-minute clip to be sent to his supporting churches every month. I want to show it on Mission Sunday to keep the work in Haiti ever before our people. It would at least raise awareness and maybe prick someone's heart for the ministry.

I video the guys and one Haitian wearing a Charlotte Hornet tank top as they begin pulling the broken roof pieces of roof off of the ladies house. This Haitian guy, who looked like a perfect NFL specimen, pushed some of our guys out of the way so he could pull away the roof section. I can only imagine what it must have been like when that section landed on her house during the tornado.

IMO really needs a boom truck to lift heavy things like roof trusses, light poles, and put generators into place. It takes so much manpower to do the simple things that one truck and an operator could do. I watched though the lens of the video camera as the roof finally falls to the ground. Herb tells everyone to take a break. Pastor John and I are heading back, and I talk Buster and Greg into coming back with us. We stopped at a couple of places to do some more video promos. The other guys stayed to finish the real work. When I looked at them soaking wet from the heat, I felt sorry for them having to stay. I know that this is what they came to Haiti for—to make a difference in at least one person's life for eternity. But, why so hot Lord? More tears as we ride down the broken road.

5:00 p.m.

Once back at the compound we found out that the crew that stayed in Bois Léger had not returned. We're starting to be a little bit worried. They were only two hours behind the crew that came back early. Lord, please protect them.

5:30 p.m.

The crew finally arrived from Bois Léger, whipped and tired, and exhausted from the heat and humidity. Earl says he has sore places on parts of his body he didn't even know he had. Rick is walking gingerly. Rick hasn't worn long pants for this long in his whole life. The lady's roof is finished, and they are making plans to go back and get the framing done on the school. Jimmy says that if they can just get the structural sections up, then someone else will have to put the tin roof on it. They all wish IMO had a boom truck. Maybe the Lord will lay it on someone's heart and make it a reality.

8:30 p.m.

Dinner is over, and some of the guys are getting supplies ready for the next day's construction project. Everyone else heads to our rooms and to the showers. Rick, Ronnie, Dad, and I are packing to go home. The rest of the guys will be heading back Monday. Our flight leaves at 9:20 a.m., but because the roads and traffic are so bad, we have to leave the compound at 6:00 a.m. for the 15-mile trip. As we walk back to our rooms, you can hear Ronnie singing, "I'm leavin' on a jet plane, I don't know when I'll be back again."

9:30 p.m.

I have almost finished packing and getting all my gadgets and hair care products put in my luggage. Dad has been packed for hours. He is leaving all his suits and clothes for the Haitian pastors. He told me, "See, Boy, if you didn't wear all that crazy stuff with the torn up jeans, *you* would have some clothes to leave too."

It has been a lot of fun getting to know the team; they are an amazingly talented group of guys. They are what servants are supposed to be. I hope we can send team after team down here. This trip has taken a toll on all of us physically but even more so mentally. It has been rough on Dad. He said tonight that this trip will probably be his last time in Haiti. He's passing the baton to me now.

No one can prepare themselves for Haiti; you have to experience it. Then while you are experiencing it, you can't wait to get home. Home to the normal. Is there anything normal in Haiti? The daily struggles that Pastor John and Joyce endure are really forever endless. The guys told me they can't wait to get to heaven to see John's and Joyce's reward. Their mansion will be tremendous. I feel in my heart that if John and Joyce had that reward now, they would somehow find a way to give it to the Haitians. The work here must go on and on and on, through every pothole, every windstorm, every hungry child, every homeless, and displaced person. Every day there is more to do, more to give out, more to build, more to repair. I think back again to Ms. Joyce's statement, "Is there ever enough?" Will there ever be enough? More tears.

P.S.: My trip to Haiti has impacted me in so many ways that only eternity will tell the whole story. When people ask me if I want to go back, I answer NO! I try to explain to them Haiti is not a place you want to return to like Hawaii or California. But as long as there is a need that I or my congregation can help with, I am willing to return and go back as many times as needed. I know because of this trip I will always have a heart for missions, especially the Haitian people. I long to see one more little boy look at me with those big eyes, high five me, and hear him say, "My man!"

Pastor Wesley Pritchard with John and Joyce in front of IMO's school building at Boutin donated by Fayetteville Community Church in Fayetteville, NC.

CHAPTER 24

IMO's Exciting Plans
for the Future

*. . . For the LORD your God will bless you in all your
harvest and in all the work of your hands, and your
joy will be complete. Deuteronomy 16:15 (NIV)*

ONE OF THE most frequently asked questions that Joyce and I get lately is, "Do you have any plans for retirement in the near future?" It is not an unusual question since I just turned 70 in February 2013, and Joyce is close behind. Retirement sounds peaceful and appealing. Maybe we could head back to the beautiful mountains of West Virginia, where I could hunt and fish and play a little golf and learn to relax all over again. I could even pastor a small church, with a small congregation; just big enough to keep me busy and out of Joyce's hair. Of course, Joyce says there is no way that would ever work: "You would be in a building program before the first year was finished!"

The truth is: God has not shown us our retirement plan just yet. Instead, God has shared with us His plans to increase our ministry here in Haiti in ways we never dreamed were possible. Let me share with you some of those plans.

When Joyce and I first came to Haiti, we had the privilege of meeting a wonderful couple by the name of George and Christine Braidwood, whose ministry was working with the deaf and sharing with them the Gospel of Jesus Christ. They ministered out of a run-down building in downtown Port-au-Prince loaned to them by the government. This area of town is still commonly referred to as the "slum district." Every time it rained, the building was flooded with water, which brought in all kinds of debris and mud.

We became good friends and helped each other out in any way we could when situations arose. We went out to eat together, prayed together, and shared our problems together. George was a whiz at computers, and he helped me set up my office computer that brought IMO into the 20th century, as far as technology was concerned.

Through the support of individual donations and churches, the deaf ministry grew, and George and Christine were able to expand their ministry. The deaf school moved from the "slum district" downtown to Bon Repos (place of peace), a village about an hour away from Port-au-Prince. At Bon Repos, their ministry grew and eventually covered over 12 and one-half acres of land housing 13 buildings. With Bon Repos being only a 30-minute drive from our headquarters, we kept in touch with them throughout the years, visiting back and forth to each of our homes.

In 2004, we were saddened to hear that George and Christine were retiring after 30 years of ministry in Haiti and heading back to the States permanently. George had hired another couple we were friends with, Steve and Judy Revis, originally from North Carolina, to run the school.

Steve was in the well drilling business, and he and Judy lived with George and Christine on the deaf school property. Steve went out drilling wells or working on some agriculture or building project, while Judy stayed and helped Christine out with the school. I had helped Steve get a well drilling rig through Haiti customs at the docks at St. Marc, Haiti, and he had drilled a well for us at Jean-Rabel in the northwest part of Haiti at our church and school there.

One evening in November 2010, around 6:00 p.m., Steve Revis came by my office at our headquarters to return some extra casing I had given him to drill the well out at Jean-Rabel. We visited for a while, getting caught up on what had been happening in our lives for the past few months. I told him that we had been actively looking for some land south of Delmas around Léogâne to build a youth camp.

To my surprise, Steve said, "If you are looking for some land, I know where there is some vacant property out at Bon Repos."

I knew the Bon Repos area well, and I couldn't imagine where in the world he was talking about. He gave me a big grin, because he knew I was familiar with the property he was talking about.

I said, "You're not talking about the deaf school property are you?"

Steve said, yes, that was the property he was talking about, and it had been vacant for four or five years. I knew that the school had eventually closed in 2008 because of too many problems, but I guess I thought it would eventually reopen. Steve relayed to me that there were no plans to reopen the school, and now, George and Christine had been thinking about selling the property. Wow! Wouldn't it be great, I thought, if we could work some type of a deal with them?

The next day, Steve and I drove out to Bon Repos, and we walked all over the 12 and one-half acres, examining the buildings and really checking out the property. Even though I had been there several times over the years, we had visited mainly in George's private residence. I was beginning to get a little excited; no, that's not exactly true. I was getting excited BIG TIME! I was picturing so many things happening on this property that it staggered my mind.

After the tour of the grounds, I told Steve that I was definitely interested. I asked him to call George to see if he was interested in talking to me about selling the property, and if he was, then have him call me. The following day, Steve called George and Christine in North Carolina, where they had retired in their hometown of Czar. And later on that evening, I received an Instant Message on the computer from George.

After our hellos, I gave George a general outline of the plans we had for the property. When I was finished, George said he would have to consult with his board of directors and some of the pastors who had been supporters of the school over the years. Let me explain here that, although the school had been supported by many churches over the years, the school and the property were actually owned by George and Christine. When the school property at Bon Repos was bought, George and Christine were careful to put it in their name. After paying for the land and paying for the building materials and labor, too many organizations had lost their property when they had short-cut the long, governmental purchasing process by putting their property in a local individual's name. Many times that local individual took over the property and made the organization get out.

George and I chatted for a few minutes, getting caught up on current activities. Then, eventually, we returned to the topic of the property. I told George to go ahead and consult with those he needed to talk with, but meanwhile, we would continue to look for property, as we were anxious to move ahead with our plans for the youth camp. As we were saying our goodbyes, George typed *"You don't have to continue your search for property."*

Stunned, I typed back, "What do you mean?"

George replied, "After talking with Steve today, Christine and I began praying about what we should do with the property, and we both got the same answer from God. He said to give IMO that property."

If my arms had been long enough to reach Czar, North Carolina, I would have given George and Christine a great big bear hug right then and there! I couldn't wait to tell Joyce the good news.

So, as you can see, retiring is out of the question for Joyce and me. There is much work to do at our new facility in Bon Repos. We just completed a 3,600-foot-long stonewall, ten feet tall, around the property. Just as I have previously stated, in Haiti, a wall is a must. When the earthquake hit in 2010, there was armed security stationed at Bon Repos or else the property would have been taken over by the "tent" people who had lost their homes. And, while we were building the wall, we removed the old damaged roof material of the overseers quarters located just right inside the main gate. We have plans to make an office out of this building. Our long-term plans are to bring an American couple to Haiti to help run this facility. Most of the other buildings are in decent condition—for Haiti, that is. And as money and time permits, updating and repairs will be made.

With so much property at our disposal, lots of plans began to formulate in our minds as to what was the best use of this special property. Of course, there will be a youth camp and training center for the youth, where there will be spiritual training, music, preaching, and teaching. And no youth camp is complete without having a recreation area for the kids to play soccer, basketball, volleyball, and, hopefully, baseball. Also, we plan to have a vocational training center with a full-time teaching staff offering courses in plumbing, electrical, welding, auto mechanic, carpentry, agriculture work, computer, and office skills. We plan to have classes for teaching nutrition and food preparation.

The Bon Repos facility already has a dormitory that sleeps over 200 people, and we plan to hold our pastor seminars and our yearly conventions here. When money permits, we hope to build more dormitories. Recently during conventions and pastor seminars at our headquarters, we have been so crowded that many of our people had to sleep on the ground. And we have no more vacant land there to expand. Also, there are plans for a huge dining hall and kitchen. When our people come to the seminars and conventions, we have to feed them since there are no restaurants available. And even if there were, the people couldn't afford to purchase food for several days.

Bon Repos is about 13 miles from our headquarters. Without a lot of traffic, it takes only 30 minutes to get there. Conveniently located on new roads being built in all directions, Bon Repos is the gateway to many of our schools and churches.

Another plan for Bon Repos is to build a 5,000-seat tabernacle on the back of the property to accommodate all our members who come to our revivals, conventions, and seminars. We plan to have permanent staff teachers who have graduated from our Bible school and teachers who can train praise and worship leaders and musicians. Along with our permanent staff, we hope to bring trained teachers from the States to Haiti for additional instruction in all phases of our training programs.

Building housing for the elderly is something we have recently started in our Boutin area. Currently, we have built 16 prefab houses that are approximately 12 ft. x 28 ft., with two bedrooms, living area, and a four-foot porch. The parsonages we build for the pastors at Perisse and Cassis are a little bit bigger at 32 ft. x 24 ft. and 14 ft. x 28 ft. respectively. The need for housing is great. Elderly people who have no family to take care of them are forgotten and die, due to starvation and exposure. In our elderly village in Boutin, we plan to build a kitchen in the center of the housing community with a permanent staff to feed these elderly. Since the houses have no bathrooms or water, we plan to build community bathrooms and provide a water supply. We are currently building these houses on site, but at Bon Repos, we plan to have a structure where we can assemble these prefab houses and transport them to wherever they are needed for the elderly. We hope, also, to have a training program for Haitians on how to build these houses.

For some time, now, we have been thinking about broadcasting our church services. We have been granted a license to build and operate our own radio station through the local Haitian government organization of Conatel. We now have room at Bon Repos to make this dream come true. We plan to play Haitian gospel music and air some of our conventions or seminars. This is a major undertaking, but finally, Haiti is joining the technology world, and we feel the time is ripe to launch this ministry. Even now, you can drive through the country areas and see a cyber cafe with a satellite on its roof running off of a generator. We want to bring in gifted people from the States to train the local people of IMO to operate this radio station.

A project that is near and dear to Joyce's heart is the modern medical clinic we plan to construct to minister to the needs of over 200,000 people still displaced and living on the hills behind our property at Bon Repos. Currently, we have medical teams coming in and providing health care for many of our congregations, but the need for a larger medical facility than the one we have at Boutin grows each day.

There are no plans for Bon Repos to replace our headquarters at Delmas, but it will be a great addition to our facility for our organization to enable us to minister to so many more Haitians. Eventually, we may move our Bible school from Delmas to Bon Repos, simply because there would be more room and facilities to teach more students.

The work at Bon Repos is keeping us busy, but ministering to the wonderful people of Haiti is our first calling. In March 2011, we dedicated our 44th church at Blanchard. It was a church that we rebuilt due to massive earthquake damage in 2010. Pastor Phil Fannin, from King's Way Church in Ashland, Kentucky, came with a group from his church to be with us during the dedication. His group painted the church and built all the benches for the church congregation and choir.

Recently, we dedicated our 45th church at Cassis, which was also a rebuild because of the 2010 earthquake. Paul Boggess, Billy Boggess, and Chad Robinson came to help us celebrate the dedication. These men represented Pastor Jim Boggess, who pastors Faith Christian Fellowship Church in Buffalo, West Virginia.

While training and providing physical needs for the people is all great and good, we still have 207 brush arbors that need permanent buildings. Of these 207 brush arbors, 25 or 30 of those areas need schools.

Our ultimate goal for all our churches is to enable them to become financially independent of IMO, although still under our direction and guidance. It is our desire that with proper skills training in our new facility at Bon Repos, our students can go back to their home areas, earn a living, and become tithing members of their congregations. When a church becomes financially independent of IMO and can pay its own pastors and workers, IMO will be able to spend that money building more churches and training more students.

Carrying out all the plans we have for Bon Repos is more of a challenge than we have ever had in any building program in Haiti. The magnitude and breath of this undertaking is mindboggling and downright scary. But the driving force to completing this challenge is the results that will be obtained when these various ministries are in operation. Our faith leads us to believe that many precious souls will be harvested into the Kingdom of God because of the work ministries at Bon Repos.

As I reflect over the last 36 years of our ministry in Haiti, I can truly testify to God's power and presence in our lives and those of our Haitian brothers and sisters. Today, IMO is educating and feeding over 5,000 children daily. There have been 45 churches planted, and more than 207 brush arbor church stations now exist with a membership totaling over 150,000 at this writing. We are educating new pastors in our Bible school where more than 8,000 students have received diplomas since 1985. Many of these students are now pastors and are ministering in our churches. We have a medical clinic that Joyce oversees which treats over 10,000 patients a year. And it all began at the altar where Joyce and I first surrendered our desires and our wills to God's ordained plan for us.

Haiti's needs are great. IMO's needs are great, but we serve a God who is greater than all our needs. ***Praise His Name!***

Building a 3,600-foot long, ten-foot tall wall was the first step to securing the 12½ acres of land and buildings at Bon Repos.

These are some of the buildings already located at Bon Repos. Future plans are to build a 5,000-seat church, modern medical clinic, youth camp, radio and TV station, and a training center for youth evangelism.

Epilogue

Peacemakers who sow in peace reap a harvest
of righteousness. James 3:18 (NIV)

*O*N JUNE 2010, our beloved daughter, Cindy, went to be with our
Lord. Each day Joyce and I thank God for the 49 years we were
privileged to have Cindy in our lives. How often I have preached that
faith is not faith until it is put to a test, and it is all you have left. In
this matter, our faith is all we have left and all that we need. From the
moment we dedicated our lives to Christ, we have trusted God in all
that came our way. The Haitians have a proverb that says: "God is an
adult; He does what He wants to." We accept this as God's will for
her and for us too. In this, we completely trust God. It is as simple as
that: we trust God.

To Cindy, Thoughts from Joyce, Faithe Ann, and John

What a beautiful baby you were! As your mother and
I held your tiny body in our arms, we could hardly
believe we created you. You grew into a lovely young
toddler whose stubbornness and determination were

your worst and best qualities. When your sister, Faithe, came along, you were truly her big sister. You were always protecting, caring, and supporting her in everything she did, and you were her all-around best friend. And, then, there was the fighting between you two, daring one another not to cross the line on either of your sides in the back seat of our car when we took trips. Then when you went on to Hair Styling School after you graduated, I can still hear the two of you giggling out loud in the middle of the night while you were cutting Faithe's hair, because that's when you had your greatest inspirations for hair designs.

What a lovely young woman you became who so graciously and willingly gave up her school, her friends, and her home to travel far away to a land not quite so pleasant as home. We were amazed at how quickly you adapted and fell in love with all the people around you. Your being able to speak the French/Creole language was such a tremendous help to us, and we were proud when you used your talents to teach Haitians the English language.

What good times we all shared together being with your family and Faithe's family. And, having the love of our beautiful grandchildren is a blessing from God. Precious family memories. As you and Shay (our son-in-law) gave so generously to support our ministry in Haiti, it meant the world to us. You and Shay helped drill wells, you helped build schools and school kitchens, you sponsored children in our school programs, and you endlessly gathered supplies to send to Haiti.

Cindy, you were so much like your father. You were a planner who always had a Plan A backed up by a B, C, and D plan if A didn't work. You always found a way to make things work out, because you could see the vision for IMO, and you wanted to be a big part of it, even if you lived thousands of miles away. We know that your legacy of love for your family and extended family in Haiti will continue on through Shay and then Samira, your beautiful daughter, who has your jovial laugh and love of people.

On the eve of your passing, you drove hard and long from Alexandria, Virginia, to Branson, Missouri, to get to hear me preach on Sunday night. You loved to sit in the audience and "Amen" my sermons, and I loved to hear your Amens! I will never forget the last night we had together as we sat in the restaurant, when you came over and sat down beside me and reached over and patted my leg. As I write this, tears fill my eyes. My heart was so full of joy, knowing how much we loved you. We will never be able to sit down and eat together as a family again on earth, but we rejoice in knowing that it is not over yet. There is going to be a banquet in heaven one day where we will all sit around our family table, fellowshipping for eternity.

Now you are with someone you love even more than your earthly family, and as you use to always say when you walked through our door, "I'm home at last." We know God will take good care of you until we meet again.

Remember, Cindy, we miss you so much every day. When our work on earth is done and we have finished our course, we will join you in heaven and have one big family reunion where we will never have to say goodbye again.

In Closing

Since I began writing this book, the view from the observation deck of our four-story building has changed. The sun still sets in the west, falling into the sea, but now during the day, crumbled buildings and white tent cities dominate the landscape. Even from this high-up position, the poverty and destruction cannot be hidden. Displaced people are everywhere with nothing to do and no place to go.

Our work is not finished here in Haiti. It will not be finished until God tells us it is time to leave. My mind races to and fro, sorting out what has to be done next and determining what best can be done with the resources we have. As I have said before, there is no time to stop and feel sorry for ourselves because we have been dealt several bad blows in the last few months. Instead, it's time to gear up, put on the full armor of God and get back to fighting the battle God has chosen for us to fight, for there is much to do to bring the Haitian people to the Kingdom of God. It's not our battle but His, and He has already won!

Paul tells us in 1 Corinthians it was his job to plant the seeds, Apollo's job to water, and God's decision to give the increase. At IMO, we firmly believe it is our job to plant the seeds and our supporters' job to water that seed. *And, forever, we must remember: it is God who gives the increase.*

Hanson Family Photos

John with daughters Faithe and
Cindy, circa 1970, Alexandria, VA.

Right to left: Cindy Hanson Sheikh, Joyce
holding Samira Sheikh, Shamim Sheikh,
and Faithe Claxton. Back row, left to right:
Rebecca Claxton, Gabriel Claxton, and John.

Faithe Hanson Claxton, Joyce Hanson,
and Cindy Hanson Sheikh

The Hanson Brothers, left to right:
Charlie, Bill, David, and John—
John's favorite fishing buddies.

IMO's Headquarters at Delmas

This is a view from the 4th story observation deck of IMO's largest church and school at Delmas.

This 4-story structure houses medical supplies on the first floor, guest quarters on the second floor, an apartment for John and Joyce on the third floor and an observation deck and office for John on the fourth floor.

A beautiful sight is containers being unloaded into the 14,000 sq. ft. warehouse building, bringing lots of food, clothing, medical, and building supplies to IMO to distribute to IMO's churches and schools.

The maintenance building at the beginning of a new day. The main gate is to the right of the photo and you can see the mountains in the background.

IMO Haitian Churches

Located in the central plateau of Haiti, this brush arbor church at Locaret with its dirt floors and canvas roofing is typical of many of the stations waiting for a more permanent structure.

This newly built IMO church at Cassis was constructed with donations from Faith Christian Fellowship located in Buffalo, WV. Associate Pastor Paul Boggess from FCF attended the dedication.

IMO Haitian Schools

Lunch time at Boutin School. IMO feels it is very important to feed the children as this is the only meal many of the students will get each day.

A typical kitchen where the food is prepared for the students each day consists of cooking pots and burners.

School children from Blanchard I school receive their
"Gifts of Love" Christmas shoe boxes from churches
who support IMO. Their smiles say it all!

Pastor Martha Joly, second lady from left, from Thomonde Brush Arbor
Church, poses with her students outside their brush arbor school.

IMO Supporters and Volunteers—The Lifeblood of IMO

Dr. Jon Sullivan from Gallipolis, Ohio, listens to the heart beat of a child at Boutin.

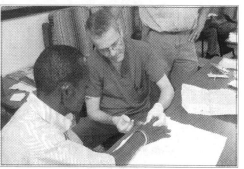

Dr. Jim Mears sutures a cut finger on IMO employee Estime.

A work team headed by Gary Reynolds from The Tabernacle Church in Danville, Virginia, putting a new roof on IMO's Boutin Church after the earthquake in 2010.

Pastor Darrell Huffman, from New Life Church in Huntington, WV, with John and Joyce at the compound in Delmas. Pastor Huffman was a guest speaker at the Haitian Pastor's Seminar.

Mark Unicume seeing his gifts in action with the children at Boutin during lunch time.

John, Tim Case and Roger Ewing from White Oak Worship Center, Blairs, Va.

Buster Livengood, Ronnie Goodman, Greg Renfrow and Rick Salyer built six metal doors for Bon Repos.

John and Joyce with Bill and Paul Boggess and Chad Robinson.

Dr. Jon Sullivan, (4th from left standing) from Lighthouse Assembly of God Church in Gallipolis, Ohio, with his medical team that consists of medical doctors, dentists, optometrists, dental hygienists, physician assistants, and nurses.

*John looking over the new housing at Boutin built by Bruce Hughes
and his work crew from White Oak Worship Center, Blairs, VA.*

*John operating a forklift loading food and water into a
transport truck to distribute to earthquake victims.*

*Long time supporters Pastor Ken Pritchard
and wife, Lillian, from Fayetteville
Community Church, Fayetteville, NC.*

*Faithful supporter Pastor Tommy Bates,
from Family Church, Independence,
KY, with John and Joyce.*

About the Writer

CHRISTINE BARBETTI-FEAMSTER received her Bachelor of Science degree in Journalism from Texas Christian University, Fort Worth, Texas. She has written feature articles for numerous newspapers and for *Aura Magazine*, Fort Worth, Texas.

Although writing a book was never a goal or desire for her, the opportunity to have a small part in such a tremendous ministry was something she felt was a privilege and honor to do. Having grown up in the beautiful Appalachian mountain area in West Virginia, she easily identifies with John's and Joyce's childhood.

She is married to Alexander Feamster, and they live in the Dallas-Fort Worth area where they own a rental property business. When business permits, they spend the rest of their time in their log home in Christine's hometown of Caldwell, West Virginia. She also enjoys spending time with her three grandchildren, Anthony, Nina, and Dante.

End Notes

1. West Virginia Office of Miners' Health Safety and Training, *A Brief History of Coal and Safety Enforcement in West Virginia*, http://www.wvminesafety.org/History.htm (February 29, 2012).

2. West Virginia – USA Geology, *History of West Virginia Mineral Industries – Coal*, http://www.wvgs.wvnet.edu/www/geology/geoldvco.htm (July 16, 2004).

3. WVa-USA.com, *The Birth of the Coal Industry*, http://wva-usa.com/history/mthope/coal.php (Copyright © 1999-2001).

4. Wikipedia, The Free Encyclopedia, *History of Haiti*, http://en.wikipedia.org/wiki/History_of_Haiti (February 12, 2012). This is the primary source for all history on Haiti.

5. Wikipedia, The Free Encyclopedia, *Hurricane Allen*, http://en.wikipedia.org/wiki/Hurricane_Allen (February 2, 2012).

6. BRnow.org, The Official Website of The Biblical Recorder, *Haiti Missionaries Ask, 'Why (not) Me?'* http://www.brnow.org/News/January-2010 (January 28, 2010).